NADIA SAWALHA
Fabulous Family Food

NADIA SAWALHA
Fabulous Family Food

Easy, delicious recipes you'll cook again and again

Food photography by **Mark Adderley**

MACMILLAN

First published 2014 by Macmillan
an imprint of Pan Macmillan,
a division of Macmillan Publishers Limited
Pan Macmillan, 20 New Wharf Road,
London N1 9RR
Basingstoke and Oxford
Associated companies throughout the world
www.panmacmillan.com

ISBN 978-1-4472-6662-4

Food photography by **Mark Adderley**

Portrait photography by **Nicky Johnston**

Hair and make-up by **Simone Vollmer**

Clothes styling by **Fiona Parkhouse**

Food styling by **Julia Alger and Rob Allison**

Food styling on pages 2, 4, 9, 26, 40, 46, 58, 81, 112,
114 bottom centre, 150, 198 by **Clare Greenstreet**

Props and styling by **Miranda Loughlin**

Design by **Lucy Parissi**

All personal photographs are the author's own, or
provided by the author's family.

Printed in Italy by Rotolito Lombarda SpA

Visit **www.panmacmillan.com** to read more about
all our books and to buy them. You will also find
features, author interviews and news of any
author events, and you can sign up for
e-newsletters so that you're always first to hear
about our new releases.

This book is for my beautiful girls, Issy, Fleur, Maddie and Kiki-Bee. I love you with all my heart.

Note on Ingredients
Eggs: All eggs used in the recipes are medium unless otherwise stated.
Butter: Where I haven't specified salted or unsalted butter in a recipe, you can use either.
Grating Lemons: A few of my recipes call for grated lemon. Make sure you grate lightly so you don't get any of the pith, which will make the recipe bitter.

CONTENTS

Food is my first love

Well, apart from my kids, dog, guinea pigs and fella – just not necessarily in that order. (Guinea pigs must always come first!) I love buying it, eating it, smelling it, looking at it, reading, writing and talking about it, and of course I love cooking it. Ahhh, what a joy!

To cook something gorgeous for those I love (even for those I only like), is to utterly lose myself in my kitchen. Sometimes if I want something really show-offy I'll happily spend hours tinkering away getting everything just so. But that's only 'sometimes' . . . because most of the time, what with the chaotic nature of modern family life, I just want and need to get gorgeous-tasting food on the table with as little fuss and nonsense as possible.

We all know great family food cooked simply is a recipe for success in any busy household . . . And I don't know about your house, but mine is insanely busy from the minute the dog lands on my head at the crack of dawn begging for her brekkie, the husband asks for the umpteenth time whether I can rustle up that lovely 'thing you do with bacon and avocado', right through till 2 a.m. when one of the teenagers will ring up for Mum and Dad's mini-cab service – invariably expecting a late night snack tucked into a Tupperware container as an accompaniment!

So, with all my family and friends to feed, my weekly food columns to invent for and numerous TV cookery shows to perform on, I'm pretty much cooking round the clock! Hence I have a whole host of recipes at my fingertips that I've tested and re-tested and that I'm now very happy to share with you lucky lot.

By turning the page you will be opening the door into my very own family kitchen where I've prepared a foodie answer to each and every one of your domestic culinary prayers. Promise!

If you've had the day from hell and fallen through the door half-starved with a famished family baying for your blood, I have a recipe to save you.

If you've forgotten that Auntie Gladys is coming round for tea and it's only her 'Coo-ee' at the door that's jogged your memory, I have a recipe to save you.

Even if you've had a slobbing-around-in-your-pyjamas day (yeah right, how often does that happen?!) and the kids have turned up with friends home for tea, never fear for I also have a recipe to save you.

As my hubby once said when he had to fend for himself and the kids in the kitchen for a week whilst I was away – 'I wish I had some quick-fix recipes ready at my fingertips'.

And that's precisely what this book is about. Whatever your family's culinary needs are, this lovingly put together book will hold your hand and guide you through over one hundred fabulous foodie answers to your prayers. So come on, put your pinny on and let's get cookin'!

NO-FUSS
FOOD

Fuss: *verb* show unnecessary or excessive concern

Synonym worry; fret; be agitated; be worried; take pains; make a big thing out of

Fussing in the kitchen is an accusation that people who don't know how to cook level at those of us who do know how to cook. It's a way of making out that we want to be stressed, that for some reason we want to be the centre of attention when all we're really doing is trying to satisfy the grumbling tummies of impatiently hungry family members and friends.

How many times have you heard someone say 'no need to fuss', or 'don't worry, I don't want anything too fussy', or 'why all the fuss and nonsense? It's only dinner!'?

If I'm honest, the only fuss in my household is the fussiness of my diners! So consider this chapter your suit of armour, designed to protect you from any accusation of being a 'fuss' in the kitchen. Knowing you have a handful of recipes up your sleeve that you can rely on, that you don't need to fret, worry, or make a big thing out of, is one of family life's greatest comforts. By the end of this chapter you'll be the proud owner of some wonderfully easy tasty recipes that you can cook any day of the week. These are the kinds of dishes you can call on for those evenings when you just want to pop open a nice cold bottle of something fizzy, get your comfies on and rustle something up that will keep everyone happy (and quiet) whilst you kick back and have the evening YOU wanted!

Whether it's a simple supper recipe for those annoying we-thought-we'd-just-pop-in friends who turn up at your door, a heart-warming midweek meal that all the family (even the picky eaters) will love, or better still, a romantic meal for two (your luck's in!) – I guarantee, whatever the scenario, you'll find the recipe to cater for your needs right here.

So how about gorgeously creamy cheese gnocchi, terrifically tasty tandoori chicken, or super savoury bread and butter pudding? These are just a few of the delights that'll be coming your way in this chapter. So, get your oven gloves on and let those corks start popping! By the time you've served up these dishes, the only fuss being made will be of you!

SESAME PORK ESCALOPES

My girls *love* to cook this dish because they *love* to get messy. Luckily for them, Mum is the messiest cook in the world so consequently doesn't give a flying banana how bad the kitchen gets. Go on, let your 'little angels' make a mess too!

Serves 4

4 pork loin steaks, all fat removed

juice of ½ lemon

large handful of plain flour

salt and pepper

2 free-range eggs, whisked

breadcrumbs made from 4 slices of bread

zest of 1 lemon

3 tbsp sesame seeds

handful of chopped flat-leaf parsley

2 tbsp freshly grated Parmesan (optional)

½ red chilli, finely chopped (optional)

vegetable oil for frying

Put the pork steaks between two pieces of clingfilm and gently flatten with a rolling pin. Rub lemon juice over them. Using three shallow bowls, put the flour in one and season well, then put the egg in another, and finally mix the breadcrumbs, lemon zest, sesame seeds, parsley, Parmesan and chilli (if using) together in the third. Season the pork, then dip in the flour, then the egg and then the breadcrumbs. Put the breaded pork into the fridge until ready to cook.

Heat a good couple of glugs of oil in a large frying pan and gently fry the escalopes for 2–3 minutes each side, until light golden brown on the outside and cooked through to the middle. Serve with spaghetti tossed in olive oil and chopped fresh tomatoes or with sauté potatoes or rice.

IT'S-COLD-OUTSIDE CASSEROLE (SPICY BEANS AND SAUSAGES)

We always have lots of friends and family round on Bonfire Night and I make this every year for all the grown-ups! The kids won't touch it, of course! So for them it's hot dogs round the fire and piles of toasted marshmallows.

Serves 4–6

2 tbsp vegetable oil

8 pork sausages

8 pork chipolatas

8 mini chorizo sausages

2 large onions, sliced

10 garlic cloves, peeled and quartered

2 red chillies, finely sliced (leave out the seeds if you don't want it too fiery or swap for red pepper if you don't want any heat at all)

2 tsp ground cumin

2 tsp allspice or mixed spice

1 heaped tbsp tomato purée

3 x 420g cans baked beans

salt and black pepper

In a large, heavy-bottomed casserole pan, heat the oil and gently fry the pork sausages, chipolatas and chorizo sausages until browned, then set aside. In the same pan, fry the onions and garlic until soft. Add the chillies and spices and fry gently until they release their aroma. Add the tomato purée and fry for a minute or two, stirring all the time. Pour in the beans, stir well together and simmer, uncovered, for 15 minutes, stirring from time to time.

Add the sausages and chipolatas, give everything a good stir and make sure it's heated through thoroughly. Then call the crowds – it's ready!

PS How about some garlic bread and jacket potatoes too?

CHEEKY CREAM AND CHEESE GNOCCHI

This is the dish Mark and I love to indulge in when we feel like a wee bit of midweek naughtiness . . . cream and cheese naughtiness that is!

Serves 4

400g gnocchi

250g broccoli

100g smoked lardons (or streaky bacon)

knob of butter

1 garlic clove, crushed

4 tbsp light cream cheese

1 tsp mustard

150ml semi-skimmed milk

salt and black pepper

150g grated strong cheese, plus extra (optional) for topping

Cook the gnocchi according to packet instructions and steam the broccoli until it's just tender.

While all that is going on, fry the lardons in a hot non-stick pan until nice and crispy, then remove with a slotted spoon and put to one side. Wipe out the pan with some kitchen paper and heat a little butter in it. Fry the garlic until it is softened. Next, stir in the cream cheese, mustard and milk. Add salt and black pepper and stir until it's smooth. Add the grated cheese.

Toss the gnocchi and broccoli into the sauce and add the bacon. Serve with extra cheese on top, if you fancy and you're NOT on a DIET!

NO-FUSS TANDOORI CHICKEN

Now don't get me wrong, I love an Indian takeaway once in a while but sometimes I like to make my own and this is a guaranteed stress-free recipe!

Serves 4

4 skinless chicken thighs

4 skinless chicken drumsticks

juice of 1 lime

1 onion, grated

200ml Greek yogurt

1 tsp grated ginger

4 garlic cloves, crushed

1 tsp curry powder

1 tsp salt

1 tsp chopped fresh chilli or chilli powder

1 tsp turmeric

4 tsp paprika

TO SERVE
rice
poppadoms
1 onion, thinly sliced
1 tsp Nigella seeds (black cumin)

Slash each chicken piece three times; this is to really let the marinade permeate the meat. Mix the other ingredients together in a large bowl and then put the chicken in and stir until all the chicken is covered in the marinade. The best thing would be to leave the chicken overnight in the marinade, but if you don't have time an hour will do.

Obviously the ultimate way to cook this is on the barbecue but if you can't be fagged, arrange the chicken pieces in a roasting tin and pop into the oven at 200°C/gas 6 for half an hour until cooked through and then crisp up a bit under the grill. Charred bits make it all extra nice!

Serve with rice and poppadoms and some thinly sliced onion lightly fried with Nigella seeds.

SPAGHETTI WITH FRIED BREAD, CHILLI AND GARLIC

This dish is one of my guilty pleasures on those rare as hen's teeth nights when I have the house to myself. Yup, Sky Plus, a large glass of red and a big bowl of spaghetti with chilli-garlic fried bread . . . what more could a girl want!

Serves 4

450g spaghetti

4 tbsp olive oil

4 garlic cloves, thinly sliced

1 red chilli, finely sliced

100g coarse breadcrumbs (made from good white bread)

2 tbsp chopped parsley

salt and pepper

Cook the spaghetti according to packet instructions.

Meanwhile, heat the olive oil and fry the garlic with the chilli until light golden brown (don't overcook the garlic as, quite frankly, it will taste disgusting if you do!), then remove with a slotted spoon. Fry the breadcrumbs in the remaining oil – adding a bit more if you doubt there is sufficient to get the bread crisp – until they're lovely and crisp and golden.

Drain the spaghetti and then stir in the parsley, chilli, garlic and breadcrumbs. You may want to drizzle on a bit more olive oil. Serve immediately – easy-peasy. Season to taste.

SUPER-EASY SUPER-SEXY PRAWNS

This is my go-to recipe when I am dead on my feet and can't face cooking anything. It's so quick and easy, but utterly delish.

Serves 4

2 tbsp olive oil

1 onion, chopped

1 celery stick, very finely chopped

garlic clove, chopped

1 red chilli, finely chopped

150ml white wine

20 cherry tomatoes

salt and pepper

pinch of sugar

600g raw peeled prawns

large handful of roughly chopped fresh coriander or flat-leaf parsley

Heat the olive oil in a non-stick frying pan then cook the onion, celery and garlic until soft. Add the chilli and stir for a minute. Now pour in the wine and let it bubble until it is reduced by half. Tip in the tomatoes. Season well, add a pinch of sugar and let it all simmer away for 10 minutes.

Stir in the prawns just before serving and heat through until pink in colour, but don't boil the life out of them as they will end up tough as old boots!

Sprinkle the coriander or parsley on top and serve with a green salad and crusty bread to mop up all those lovely juices.

SCETTI AND BALLS

Or, as you and I would say, spaghetti and meatballs. If Kiki-Bee is having a play date she always asks me to make scetti and balls because, as she says, 'Most kids like scetti, Mummy.' Well, she's right, I certainly have yet to meet one that doesn't! So next time your little ones (or big ones) have friends over, treat them to these utterly delicious super-juicy, stupidly tasty meatballs and be the talk of the playground!

Serves 4

1 thick slice of bread, crust removed

a good glug of milk

300g pork mince

250g beef mince

small handful of fresh parsley

zest of 2 lemons

1 fat garlic clove

½ onion

salt and pepper

plain flour for coating

olive oil and butter for frying

pesto or tomato spaghetti or pasta shapes, to serve

Put the bread on a plate, cover it with milk and allow it to bathe for 10 minutes-ish. Now mush it up with a fork (good one to get the kids to do) and put it in a bowl with the rest of the ingredients. Season well and give everything a good mix. Heat up a frying pan, fry a teaspoon of the meat and taste, then add more seasoning if necessary (that's what they do in posh restaurant kitchens).

Then sprinkle some flour on a large plate. Wet your hands (this will stop the meat from sticking to you) and gently roll walnut sized balls of the mixture in the flour. Being gentle stops the meat compacting and the balls getting tough.

Heat a glug of olive oil and a knob of butter gently in a large frying pan. Fry the meatballs without overcrowding them for 4–6 minutes until light golden brown all over and cooked through. Don't overcook if you want them to be juicy! Serve with pesto or tomato spaghetti or pasta shapes.

SAVOURY BREAD AND BUTTER PUDDING

Don't be shocked – I promise it tastes great! And you could always rustle up a sweet one for pud if you're feeling especially naughty . . . or maybe not!

Serves 4

1 large red onion, sliced

1 tbsp vegetable oil

1 small garlic clove

30g butter, softened

½ large stick of stale French bread

14 cherry tomatoes, halved

100g smoked ham, chopped

3 large free–range eggs

500ml semi-skimmed milk

1 tsp Dijon mustard

40g Parmesan, grated

salt and pepper

60g mature Cheddar, grated

Preheat the oven to 180°C/gas 4.

Fry the onions in the oil until softened, and set to one side. Crush the garlic and mix it into the butter. Cut the French bread into thickish slices, then spread both sides of each slice with the garlic butter and arrange them in an ovenproof dish, layering with the tomatoes, ham and fried onion.

Crack the eggs into the measured milk. Add the mustard and the Parmesan, season, whisk together, then pour over the bread. Make sure that all the bread slices are wet. Leave for 5 minutes. Top with the Cheddar cheese and bake for 40 minutes until nice and golden.

DREAMY CREAMY TUNA BAKE

This is a great store-cupboard staple, one of those bung-it-all-together dishes that can save you from reaching for the takeaway menus! You can swap whatever you don't have to hand for whatever's lurking at the back of your shelves.

Serves 4–6

600g pasta pieces

salt and black pepper

50g butter, plus a bit extra for frying

1 bunch of spring onions, finely chopped

50g plain flour

500ml skimmed milk

200g extra-mature Cheddar, grated

1 red pepper, finely sliced (optional)

100g cooked peas

2 x 200g tins tuna, drained

200g tinned sweetcorn, drained

handful of chopped fresh parsley

Cook the pasta according to the packet instructions, adding salt to the water. Heat a small knob of butter in a non-stick pan and fry the spring onions in it until soft. Set aside.

Melt the rest of the butter in the same pan and stir in the flour until it forms a smooth paste. Allow to cook for a couple of minutes, then gradually pour in the milk, whisking the whole time, until it comes up to the bubble. Turn the heat down and stir until the sauce thickens.

Now throw in most of the cheese, keeping aside just enough to sprinkle on the top. Season well, using plenty of black pepper. Add the fried spring onions, red pepper (if using), peas, tuna, sweetcorn, cooked pasta and parsley. Transfer to an ovenproof dish and sprinkle the remaining cheese over the top. Grill until it's all bubbly and golden.

COMFORT
FOOD

Comforting: *verb* to soothe, console or reassure; bring cheer to

When the words 'COMFORT FOOD' are mentioned in a cookery book, television show or between foodies, they often refer to the most indulgent, bad-for-you dishes known to man. Conversation quickly settles on such delicacies as hot crumpets dripping with butter, syrupy steamed puds, sickly (for some!) sweet iced buns, lush bacon sandwiches, and on and on.

I get as much comfort from soft, sticky, creamy nursery food as the next person. But the physical pleasure of biting into a Victoria sponge, layered with cream and jam, lasts for just a few seconds (albeit great seconds) before the guilt kicks in. To comfort isn't simply about filling someone up (though it often helps) – it's about creating a state of mind. Don't get me wrong, one day I'll definitely publish the ultimate cookbook that's defined by its desire to kill us all with over-indulgence (*The Ultimate Blow-Out Cook Book!*), but for now, whilst we all have a chance to live long, eat well and prosper, my definition of Comfort Food – or Comforting Food – is as much about the people, places and happy moments a dish can remind us of as it is about the medicinal powers of taste and texture.

The recipes I've included in this section always make me think about the people I originally designed them for as they will, hopefully, make you think about the people you decide to cook them for. These dishes are ALL about the comfort we feel from happy memories, reminiscences, friendships, loves, anniversaries and celebrations.

I find comfort in creating a dish that makes other people feel safe, looked after, indulged and well fed. I know that for my husband simply fried white fish with new potatoes takes him back to the childhood comfort of being cooked for by his nan. For Dad, it may well be a dish that takes him back to his desert origins. For my eleven-year-old, Maddie, comfort is to be had in a plate of creamy mashed potatoes, whilst Kiki-Bee is happily in her comfort food zone when she is stealing fruit out of her dada's hands!

That's why I've called this chapter 'Comfort Food'– it's all about those dishes (some surprising) that if cooked at the right time, in the right way, for the right person, will give them a food experience they'll never forget. Give yourself a challenge, as you read this chapter: try finding and matching the right dish for the right person as you go!

BABY SHEPHERD'S PIES

Plain and simple but always a favourite with my brood. Now I've said mince in the ingredients, but my mum always used to make her shepherd's pie with leftover roast lamb, which I would love to do – trouble is there's never any left in my house.

Serves 4

2 tbsp sunflower oil

800g best-quality lamb mince

1 onion, finely chopped (grated if yours don't like bits)

1 garlic clove, crushed

1 tbsp plain flour

500ml beef stock

1.2kg potatoes, washed, peeled and halved

30g butter

185ml milk

salt and black pepper

200g Cheddar, grated

Heat ½ tablespoon of the oil in a heavy-based pan over a medium-high heat. Add half the lamb and cook, turning, for 3–4 minutes or until well browned then set aside. Then do the same thing all over again with the other half!

Heat the remaining oil in the pan over a medium heat and cook the onion until it is lovely and soft. Add the garlic and cook, stirring, for 1 minute or until aromatic. Sprinkle the flour over the onion mixture and cook, stirring, for 1 minute.

Gradually add the stock to the pan, stirring the whole time. Stir in the lamb. Cover and bring to a simmer over a medium-low heat. Reduce the heat to low and simmer, covered, stirring occasionally, for 20 minutes or until the sauce thickens.

Meanwhile, cook the potatoes in a large pan of salted boiling water for 25 minutes or until tender. Drain and return to the pan. Mash the potatoes until almost smooth then add the butter and milk, and mash until completely smooth. Taste and season with salt and pepper.

Divide the lamb mixture between four 6cm-deep 250ml ovenproof dishes. Spread evenly with mashed potato and lightly rough the surface and sprinkle with cheese. Pop them under a hot grill and cook until golden brown. Serve with mounds of peas (your kids can always hide them under the radiator like mine do!).

GLORIOUSLY GARLICKY CHICKEN

Come on, you know it and I know it. Nothing is quite as comforting as a house filled with the aroma of a perfectly roasting chicken. It's definitely my girls' most favourite dinner and what I cook to welcome them home, if I know they've had a tough day.

Now this recipe isn't a Sunday roast kinda chicken stuffed and served with all the trimmings. No, this is more of a midweek indulgence. So I usually serve it with nothing more than a crisp green salad and French bread so that we can mop up the pan juices with it.

PS Mushing the garlic cloves into the bread before chomping is as pretty damn close to foodie heaven as you can get.

Serves 4–6

1.7kg whole chicken cut into pieces

2 tbsp olive oil

salt and pepper

1 tbsp mixed herbs

3–4 heads of garlic, cloves separated and left unpeeled

good splash of white wine

Preheat the oven to 220°C/gas 7.

Put the chicken into a roasting tin (a tin is best for a crispy chicky), rub all over with the oil and season all over. Then sprinkle the herbs over and scatter the garlic cloves around the chicken.

Put into the oven and cook for 20 minutes at the high heat. Then take the tin out, lower the oven temperature to 180°C/gas 4 and baste the chicken with the juices. Pour the wine into the bottom of the pan, making sure you don't pour it over the chicken, and return to the oven for another 45 minutes or until the juices run clear.

Take out the breasts 20 minutes before the rest is cooked and keep warm. This will prevent them over-cooking and becoming dry.

PERFECT GREEN SALAD

Sometimes all you need to accompany a dish is a lovely crisp green salad. This goes beautifully with Gloriously Garlicky Chicken (page 35) and Super-Easy Super-Sexy Prawns (page 23).

Serves 4

1 soft round lettuce

large handful of rocket

large handful of watercress

½ cucumber, diced

1 ripe avocado, sliced

torn basil leaves, parsley, lovage, dill, or whatever herb you fancy

FOR THE VINAIGRETTE

1 dsp Dijon mustard

1 tbsp rice wine vinegar

1 tbsp sherry vinegar

8 tbsp light olive oil

sea salt (I like Maldon flaked – get me!)

black pepper

1 fat garlic clove

Start with the vinaigrette. Spoon the mustard into a large salad bowl and whisk in the vinegars, oil, salt and pepper. Peel the garlic and spear it with a fork. Now whisk the vinaigrette with the garlic-speared fork, then leave the fork and garlic sitting in the dressing until you are ready to make the salad.

When you're about to serve, give the dressing another whisk with the fork. Add all the salad ingredients to the bowl and toss!

CHICKEN FRICASSEE

We used to have a very different version of La Fricassee at school and it wasn't good! But the fried bread saved it – my love of fried bread is legendary – and I would beg, borrow and steal to get any leftover bits from the dinner ladies!

Well, I made myself a solemn promise back in that smelly school dinner hall. One day, I would right the injustice that had been meted out on all those who had been forced to eat that foul fricassee, by feeding my own brood with not just a good fricassee but a sublime one. Little did I know back then that I would be feeding so many more than just my own. *Bon appetit, tout le monde!*

Serves 4

6 chicken pieces, skin on

2 tbsp seasoned plain flour

50g butter

1 onion, finely chopped

1 tbsp tomato purée

1 glass of white wine

1 bouquet garni

250ml chicken stock

200ml double cream

2 free-range egg yolks

½ tsp caster sugar

2 tsp chopped fresh parsley

FOR THE CROUTONS

vegetable oil for frying

3–6 slices white bread (depending on how much you like fried bread)

Dry the chicken with some kitchen paper and dust with the seasoned flour. Heat the butter in a flameproof casserole dish and brown the chicken pieces on a medium heat a few at a time. Set them aside and keep them warm as you go along.

Add the onion and fry slowly. Once softened, add the tomato purée. Now pour in the wine and add the bouquet garni. Stir for 30 seconds and then let it bubble for a couple of minutes. Put the chicken back into the dish and pour the stock over. Simmer on a low heat until cooked through. This should take about 40 minutes (if you are using breasts they will take half the time, be careful not to overcook them). Remove the chicken pieces and keep warm.

Mix the double cream and egg yolks together with the sugar and a teaspoon of the stock liquid. Now pour the egg and cream mixture back into the casserole dish and heat gently (no boiling) until the sauce thickens. Serve the chicken coated with the sauce, sprinkled with parsley and the gorgeous croutons.

CROUTONS

Heat some oil in a frying pan and cut the bread into whatever shape you fancy – I like hearts. When the oil is nice and hot gently fry the bread on both sides until golden brown.

KOMFORTING KORMA BALLS

I love the title of this recipe! Oh, and they taste pretty good too.

Serves 4

500g chicken mince

4 tbsp finely chopped fresh coriander or parsley

1 tsp ground coriander

1 tsp ground cumin

salt and pepper

2 tbs plain flour

1 tbsp vegetable oil

1 onion, finely chopped

2 garlic cloves, chopped

2 tbsp korma curry paste

175ml coconut milk

500ml chicken stock

16 cherry tomatoes

1 tbsp blanched, or flaked almonds

To make the meatballs, put the mince, fresh herbs, ground coriander, cumin, a good pinch of salt and pepper into a bowl and mix thoroughly. Then wet your hands (so the meat doesn't stick to them) and shape it into walnut-sized meatballs. Roll the balls in the flour.

Heat a large non-stick frying pan and pour in the oil. Fry the meatballs, turning the whole time, until browned all over. Take out of the pan with a slotted spoon and set aside.

Add the onion to the pan and fry over a very low heat until softened, then add the garlic and cook until soft. Now add the korma paste to the onion and garlic mixture and fry over a low heat for about a minute, or until the aroma is released. Pour in the coconut milk and stock and bring it up to the bubble, then turn the heat down to low, add the meatballs and cook gently for about 10 minutes until the chicken is cooked through, but be careful not to overcook or the chicken will be dry. Add the tomatoes and cook for a couple more minutes, then scatter with the almonds before serving.

MINCED LAMB AND SPICED PASTRY PIE

This makes such a nice change from a traditional shepherd's or cottage pie and for no more effort either. And, boy, how comforting is puff pastry!

Serves 4–6

750g minced lamb

3 tbsp vegetable oil

1 large onion, sliced

4 large carrots, peeled and cubed

1 garlic clove, crushed

1 tbsp plain flour

3 tbsp tomato purée

600ml flavoursome stock

100g frozen peas

FOR THE PASTRY TOPPING

500g block puff pastry

1 tsp each of coriander and cumin seeds, dry-fried

1 free-range egg, beaten, to glaze

Heat a tablespoon of vegetable oil in a large frying pan and fry the mince in batches until browned. Remove with a slotted spoon and set to one side. Don't be tempted to cook it all at once because you will end up with boiled rather than fried meat. Yuk!

Pour the remaining oil into the same frying pan and fry the onion and carrots until softened. Stir in the garlic and fry for another minute or so. Sprinkle over the flour and cook for a minute or two before stirring in the tomato purée. Add the browned mince to the vegetables and then pour over the stock. Bring up to the boil, reduce the heat and let it all bubble and pop away for 25 minutes.

Next, spoon the vegetables and mince into your most homely rectangular pie dish. Allow to cool. You ignore this cooling bit at your peril, or your pastry will melt when you place it on top. I know this from bitter experience! Stir in the frozen peas.

Meanwhile, preheat the oven to 190°C/gas 5.

Roll out your pastry to approximately 25cm square. Sprinkle half the coriander and cumin seeds over the bottom half of the pastry then fold the pastry in half to cover them. Sprinkle the rest of the seeds over the left-hand side of the pastry and then fold the pastry in half again to cover them. Roll out the pastry to about 2cm larger all the way round than the top of your pie dish.

Use a strip of pastry to line the edge of the pie dish and brush with water. Place the remaining pastry on top and press down to seal. Brush with egg to glaze.

Cook in the oven for about 25–30 minutes, or until the filling is piping hot and the pastry is puffed and golden. Some extra steamed veg is all you need.

MEAT LOAF MUFFINS

Most children hate to share. This is a fact that any parent will know only too well. I have used this childhood failing to my advantage when trying to get the 'little darlings' to eat new things. They truly love an individual anything – they fall for it every time – so small wonder that my amazing meat loaf muffins have been a hit right from day one!

Serves 2 adults, 2 children

4 tbsp vegetable oil

1 onion, grated

1 carrot, grated

50g sage and onion stuffing, plus water to make up (or 50g breadcrumbs)

handful of fresh parsley, finely chopped

a good squeeze of tomato ketchup

1 free-range egg, beaten

500g minced pork

zest of 1 unwaxed lemon

salt and pepper

2 tomatoes, sliced thickly

Preheat the oven to 200°C/gas 6.

Heat 1 tablespoon of the oil in a large frying pan and fry the onion and carrot until they soften. This will only take a few minutes. Now put the fried vegetables into a large bowl, and add the stuffing, parsley, tomato ketchup, egg, pork and lemon zest. Give the mixture a good stir and season well.

Brush six holes of a muffin tin with a little oil and press the meat loaf mince into them. Top with the tomatoes, brushed with the remaining oil. Sprinkle a little salt on top of the tomatoes. Bake for 30–40 minutes until cooked through. Serve with mash, peas and gravy.

MAMA'S MINESTRONE SOUP

I love to imagine I'm a Sophia Loren-like domestic goddess when I'm at my stove stirring my mama's minestrone. This is perfectly possible just as long as I don't catch sight of my reflection in the kettle.

Serves 4

2 tbsp olive oil

100g smoked lardons

1 onion, finely chopped

1 garlic clove, crushed

2 carrots, peeled and finely diced

3 celery sticks, diced

½ red pepper, chopped

1 courgette, finely chopped

2 tsp tomato purée

1.25 litres beef, chicken or vegetable stock

salt and pepper

½ tsp dried oregano

100g small pasta shapes

handful of chopped cabbage

TO SERVE

4 tbsp grated fresh Parmesan

fresh basil or parsley

Put the oil into a heavy-based saucepan and fry the lardons until light golden brown then add the onion and garlic and fry until softened. Add the carrot, celery, pepper and courgette and fry until lightly browned.

Stir in the tomato purée followed by the stock, salt, pepper and oregano. Bring to the boil, add the pasta then reduce to a simmer and cook until the vegetables and pasta are just soft. Stir in the chopped cabbage and simmer until the cabbage has wilted. Serve sprinkled with lots of Parmesan and basil or parsley leaves.

STICKY SESAME SPARE RIBS

This was the most popular recipe I cooked on *Sunday Scoop*, not only for the guests on the show that day but also for the viewers! I got so many tweets and emails from people saying how delicious the ribs were that I'm afraid it went straight to my head and I have been utterly full of myself ever since. God, they are good though!

Serves 4

2kg rack spare ribs

TO SIMMER

200ml soy sauce

100g muscovado sugar

2 tbsp Chinese five-spice powder

8 whole star anise

1 red chilli, finely chopped

1 small onion, peeled

8 slices fresh ginger

FOR THE MARINADE

130ml dark soy sauce

75g light brown muscovado sugar

90ml cider vinegar

8 tbsp tomato ketchup

3 large garlic cloves, crushed

4 tbsp sweet chilli sauce

2 heaped tbsp finely grated fresh ginger

juice of 1½ limes

5 tbsp toasted sesame seeds

Preheat the oven to 180°C/gas 4.

Place the ribs in a flameproof roasting tin. Mix all of the simmer ingredients in a jug then pour them over the ribs. Add enough water to cover the ribs completely.

Bring up to the boil on the hob and then carefully put the tin into the oven to simmer for 45–60 minutes or until the ribs are tender. Top up with boiling water if it looks like they need it.

Remove from the oven and leave the ribs to cool completely in the liquid. This will take about 4 hours. Once cooled, you can leave them overnight, covered, in the fridge.

Remove the cooled rack of ribs from the poaching liquid to a chopping board, then pat dry with kitchen paper. Using a large knife, cut between the ribs to separate. Put the ribs in a single layer in a large oven dish or lipped baking tray. Mix the marinade ingredients in a bowl. Pour over the ribs, mixing well to coat generously. Cover, then leave to marinate in the fridge for as long as you have – hours or overnight if possible.

Remove the ribs from the fridge to bring up to room temperature. Heat the grill then place the ribs onto the grill pan. Pour the yummy leftover marinade from the dish into a small saucepan, bring it up to the boil and bubble for a few minutes until it thickens. Grill the ribs for 10–15 minutes until they are sticky and really nice and hot. Turn them over halfway through and brush with the marinade.

ONE-POT
WONDERS

Wonder: *noun* a person or thing regarded as very good, remarkable, or effective

As far as I'm concerned this **One-Pot Wonder** chapter is most definitely 'a thing regarded as very good'! Firstly, there's the fact that all the recipes can be cooked using just one pot (tell your partner to hang up the Marigolds). Secondly, all these recipes can be cooked using just one pot (it's such a good point I felt I needed to list it twice). And, thirdly, they're all absolutely delicious, won't cost you the earth, and won't have you slaving for hours over a hot stove.

Leaf through the next few pages of this book and you'll find the kind of dishes that will soothe your family's ills, whilst putting you (their rather fabulously important cook) firmly in their hearts and minds. In other words: cooking a One-Pot Wonder is a WIN-WIN!

Crack on with just one or two of these recipes and you will quickly discover the charm of the OPW. The OPW allows the most reluctant of cooks to feel like they've dished up an absolute masterpiece. These recipes are mini-instruction manuals on how to win friends and influence people through food! Indeed, dishes such as my succulent *Olé* Chicken are so easy that even Mark (something of a stick-a-needle-in-the-eye-rather-than-cook kind of guy) has been seen getting my pinny on (he'll kill me for that) and whipping this dish up for the kids and himself when I'm out. (Maddie has the evidence on her iPhone!)

If you fancy something a little edgier, a little spicier, something that will set the cat amongst the pigeons, then go and get your pots and pans (well, your pot and pan) out and cook up my beautiful (it's the herby dumplings that make it beautiful!) Beef Casserole. Fragrant with Middle Eastern spices and sweetened with sticky Medjool dates, it's the ultimate 'anytime-in-the-week' indulgence.

The OPW for me is a little like the magician's hat! You choose your ingredients, cut them into shape and tip them in – whilst the wow factor is all in The Reveal. One-pot wonders are about trusting your ingredients, trusting the flame – and believing they will come out the other side having had the right effect on each other. That's why when an OPW is served up it is like the finale of a magic trick. Everything has interacted and been transformed into a wonderful tasty ending!

SWEETLY SAVOURY SLOW-COOKED LAMB

This is a one-pot wonder that is not only delicious but really affordable too, because I use a shoulder of lamb, which is one of the best-value cuts you can get. Serve simply with couscous or chunks of bread, and a salad, for an alternative Sunday lunch and your family will soon forget what stuffing and Yorkshire puddings were.

Serves 6–8

5 garlic cloves, bashed (go on, bash it!)

3 red onions, chopped into chunky rings

1 tbsp ground cinnamon

1 tbsp ground cumin

1 tbsp olive oil

salt and pepper

1 shoulder of lamb (roughly 2.5kg), at room temperature

2 x 400g tins chopped tomatoes

1 tbsp brown sugar (if you don't have brown, just use caster)

16 dried apricots

500ml hot vegetable or chicken stock

60g pistachios, roughly chopped

2 tbsp chopped fresh parsley

2 tbsp chopped fresh mint

2 tbsp chopped fresh chives

Preheat your oven to 240°C/gas 8.

Put the cloves of garlic, chopped red onions, cinnamon, cumin and olive oil into a bowl and mix well with your hands. Season with a little salt and pepper before scattering on the base of a roasting dish that is big enough to take the lamb.

Season the joint with a generous amount of salt and pepper before placing on top of the vegetables. Place the roasting dish in the preheated oven and roast for 20 minutes, by which time the lamb should have turned a satisfying golden colour.

Meanwhile, put the chopped tomatoes, sugar, dried apricots and a generous amount of salt and pepper in a saucepan. Add the stock, mix the whole lot together and bring to a simmer.

Once the lamb has had its 20 minutes, remove it from the oven and carefully drain as much of the excess fat that has gathered in the bottom of the dish as possible. Pour the stock and tomato mixture around the lamb shoulder, cover the whole lot with foil and replace the dish in the oven.

Reduce the oven temperature to 170°C/gas 3 and cook for 2½ hours. During the final 30 minutes of cooking remove the foil and baste the lamb with the tomato sauce a couple of times to give it a lovely caramelized glaze.

Remove from the oven and let the dish sit for 10 minutes before scattering the chopped pistachios over the lamb shoulder and transferring it to a chopping board ready for carving. Add the chopped herbs to the sauce and mix well. Either serve the sauce on top of the carved meat, or mix the carved meat and sauce before serving. Whatever takes your fancy!

BEEF CASSEROLE WITH HERB DUMPLINGS

A classic dish, and I just couldn't stop myself from adding a couple of Middle Eastern surprises to keep the ever faithful beef casserole interesting – oh, and because I love to show off!

Serves 4–6

2 tbsp olive oil

1kg stewing beef (preferably shin), chopped into large (3cm) pieces

1 large onion, diced

2 carrots, peeled and diced into 1cm pieces

4 celery sticks, diced into 1cm pieces

2 bay leaves

8 dates, roughly chopped into small pieces

peel of 1 orange

1 heaped tablespoon tomato purée

1 glass of red wine

300ml beef stock

HERB DUMPLINGS

175g self-raising flour

60g shredded beef suet

1 bunch of parsley, finely chopped

2 bunches of chives, finely chopped

juice of ½ orange

120ml water

Preheat the oven to 170°C/gas 3.

Heat the oil in a large flameproof casserole dish over a high heat. Once hot add the beef chunks and fry until golden brown all over. If your dish isn't big enough to accommodate all of the meat in a single layer, then fry in two batches. Once the meat is nicely browned all over, remove to a plate and leave to one side.

Reduce the heat to medium and add the diced onion, carrots and celery. Fry the vegetables for 5–6 minutes until starting to soften. Add the bay leaves, dates and two 4cm strips of orange peel that can be easily removed with a peeler. Continue to fry for a further minute. Add the tomato purée and fry for a minute, stirring regularly.

Increase the heat to maximum and add the red wine. Let the wine bubble away and reduce by three-quarters. Pour in the beef stock and return the browned meat to the pan. Bring the whole lot to the boil before reducing to a simmer. Place the lid on top and put the casserole into the preheated oven. Cook for 1½ hours, by which time the meat should be tender.

While the meat is cooking, tip the flour, suet and chopped herbs into a bowl along with a generous amount of salt and pepper. Mix together with a fork. Squeeze in the juice of half the orange and about half the water. Continue to bring the mixture together with your fork, adding water as needed. You are aiming for quite a stiff dough. Divide the dough into eight, and roll into balls.

Remove the stew from the oven and take off the lid. Drop the dough balls into the stew as evenly spaced as possible. Increase the oven temperature to 190°C/gas 5 and place the dish back into the oven, without the lid. Continue to cook for a further 30 minutes, by which time the dumplings should have swollen up, absorbing plenty of the delicious gravy. Serve immediately to only your very closest friends.

CHICKEN CHASSEUR

There's one reason this dish has survived the test of time – its simple deliciousness. Warm and homely, it is the culinary equivalent of snuggling down on your favourite sofa in front of a roaring fire. Mmmmm . . .

Serves 4–6

2 tbsp olive oil

6 large chicken thighs, skin on and bone in

salt and pepper

2 red onions, roughly diced

3 rashers smoked streaky bacon, chopped into 1cm pieces

3 garlic cloves, finely chopped

250g button mushrooms, brushed clean

2 sprigs of thyme

1 heaped tablespoon tomato purée

1 large glass of white wine

150ml chicken stock

12 cherry tomatoes on the vine

4 tbsp chopped fresh parsley, to serve

Heat half of the olive oil in a large flameproof casserole dish over a medium to high heat. Dry the chicken thighs with kitchen paper and season all over. Once the oil is hot place in the pan skin side down. Fry for a few minutes, turning a couple of times, until they are golden brown all over. When your thighs (well not yours, your chickens'!) are well browned, remove them to a plate and leave to one side.

Carefully wipe your pan clean with a bit of kitchen paper before pouring in the rest of the olive oil. When the oil is hot add the red onions, bacon, garlic and mushrooms. Fry over a medium to high heat for 2–3 minutes until the vegetables and bacon start to soften and lightly colour.

Drop in the thyme sprigs and the tomato purée. Continue to fry the mixture, stirring, for a further minute before pouring in both the wine and the chicken stock. Stir all the ingredients together and bring up to the boil before reducing the heat to a simmer. Place the browned chicken thighs back into the bubbling liquid skin side up.

Cook the dish, uncovered, either in an oven preheated to 180° C/gas 4 for 30 minutes or on the hob, simmering, for 20 minutes.

Then drop in the cherry tomatoes still on the vine. Continue cooking for a further 5 minutes, in the oven or on the hob, until the tomatoes have softened but are still holding their shape.

Just before serving, scatter over the chopped parsley. Serve with lashings of creamy mash. Now it's even better . . .

SWEET POTATO CURRY

Although this dish is most definitely influenced by my love of Thai food, it isn't fiery, and is a great way to introduce your kids to the delights of curries. Even my Maddie will eat it and, believe me, that's a flaming ('scuse the pun) miracle. If you want to fire it up for the grown-ups then simply ramp up the heat of the curry powder and chuck in some fresh red chilli.

Serves 4–6

4 large chicken breasts, cut into 1cm slices

2 heaped tbsp mild curry powder

salt and pepper

3 tbsp olive oil

2 red onions, finely diced

5 garlic cloves, finely chopped

5cm fresh ginger, finely chopped

2 lemongrass stalks, trimmed and finely chopped

400ml tin coconut milk

100ml water

2 medium sized sweet potatoes, peeled and chopped into 2cm chunks

250g baby spinach

2 tbsp fish sauce

about 2 limes, juice only

Place the chicken breast slices in a bowl and sprinkle over half the curry powder along with a generous amount of salt and pepper. Mix well with a spoon so that the chicken is evenly coated by the curry powder. Leave to one side.

Heat 2 tablespoons of the olive oil in a wide saucepan over a medium to high heat. When hot, drop in the red onions, garlic and ginger. Fry the ingredients for about 3 minutes until starting to soften. Add the lemongrass and continue to stir and cook for a further 2 minutes.

Add the remaining olive oil and curry powder to the softening ingredients, increase the heat to maximum and add the chicken breast strips. Fry the ingredients together for about 2 minutes, stirring almost constantly to ensure the curry powder doesn't burn.

Pour in the coconut milk along with the water. Stir and bring to the boil, before reducing to a simmer and dropping in the sweet potato chunks. Simmer like this for about 10 minutes, by which time the sweet potato should be tender.

Add the spinach to the curry and stir it through to wilt. Remove the pan from the heat and add the fish sauce along with some of the lime juice. Taste the curry and add more lime juice to your taste.

Serve up with bowls of steaming jasmine rice.

OLÉ CHICKEN

A little bit of Spanish sunshine on a plate! The smoked paprika adds a whole other dimension and makes everything taste good. Once you've discovered it you'll be sprinkling it on everything you eat from toast to tea . . . Well maybe not tea, but you get my gist!

Serves 4

2 tbsp olive oil

8 chicken thighs, skin on and bone in

salt and pepper

1 large red onion, diced

1 red and 1 green pepper, deseeded and chopped into 2cm pieces

5 garlic cloves, finely chopped

1 heaped tbsp smoked paprika

1 heaped tbsp tomato purée

100ml dry sherry

400g tin cherry tomatoes

400g tin chickpeas, drained and rinsed

2 large handfuls of baby spinach

Heat the olive oil in a large saucepan over a medium to high heat. Dry the chicken thighs with kitchen paper and season with a generous amount of salt and pepper. When the oil is hot, add the chicken thighs to the pan, skin side down. Cook without turning for about 4 minutes by which time the skin should have turned a golden colour. Turn and brown on the flesh side for a further 2–3 minutes. If your pan is not big enough to accommodate all the chicken thighs in a single layer then cook in two batches.

When the chicken is browned, remove to a plate. Add a little more oil if necessary before adding in the red onion, peppers and garlic. Fry the vegetables for 3–4 minutes, stirring regularly until they begin to soften, then add the smoked paprika and tomato purée. Continue stirring and frying for a further minute before pouring in the sherry. Increase the heat to maximum and let the sherry reduce by three-quarters.

Tip in the cherry tomatoes and stir, so that all the ingredients are well mixed. Place the chicken thighs back into the pan skin side up. Put a lid on top and reduce the heat to a simmer. Cook like this for about 20 minutes, by which time the chicken should be cooked through. If you feel the mixture needs more liquid then just add a little water, and stir in.

After 20 minutes' cooking, tip in the drained chickpeas and stir so they are submerged in the tomato sauce. Replace the lid and cook for a further 5 minutes. Finally, remove the lid and add the spinach, mixing it in with the rest of the ingredients until it wilts.

Serve with rice or on its own.

SPICY LAMB AND BARLEY SOUP

I suppose this dish has its origins in Scotland, where they love to boil up mutton with barley to make a soup so hearty it could toss a caber. I've gone for a slightly lighter option using lots of vegetables and chicken stock, but have spiced it up with the addition of a little harissa. So Scotland and Morocco meet, and why not? Dad, this one's for you; it's right up your alley!

Serves 4

1 tbsp olive oil

200g lamb leg steak, chopped into 1cm pieces

salt and pepper

1 onion, finely diced

1 carrot, peeled and chopped into 1cm pieces

2 garlic cloves, finely chopped

1 tbsp rose harissa, plus extra to serve

700ml chicken stock

50g barley

1 courgette, trimmed and chopped into 1cm pieces

400g tin butter beans or cannellini beans, drained and rinsed

100g kale, trimmed

½ bunch of parsley, chopped

Heat the olive oil in a large saucepan over a high heat. Season the lamb pieces generously with salt and pepper. When the oil is hot, add the meat to the pan and fry over the high heat for 2 minutes.

Add the onion, carrot and garlic. Reduce the heat to medium and continue to fry for a further 3 minutes, stirring regularly. Add the harissa. Stir to mix all the ingredients before pouring in the chicken stock and barley.

Increase the heat to bring the liquid to the boil before reducing to a simmer and cooking for about 15 minutes. Add the courgette, beans and kale and stir to mix through. Simmer for a further 5 minutes, by which time all the ingredients should be deliciously soft.

Sprinkle over the parsley and serve up steaming bowls of your spicy lamb soup along with extra harissa.

NB It is easy to make this soup go further by adding a second tin of beans.

BETTY'S HOTPOT

This one's for you, Betty, for all those years of hard work entertaining us. You can find the original Betty's hotpot online and in magazines, but here is my version, with a couple of unexpected twists that I'm sure Betty would approve of.

   PS Sorry Mum, I don't mean you . . . I mean Betty from Corrie.

Serves 4–6

FOR THE HOTPOT

30g raisins

60g (-ish) butter

1kg lamb neck, chopped into large (3cm) dice

salt and pepper

2 onions, finely sliced

2 tsp ground turmeric

2 tbsp plain flour

400ml chicken or beef stock

5 tbsp Worcestershire sauce

10 slices white bread, crusts removed

mint sauce, to serve

FOR THE CABBAGE

½ red cabbage, cored and finely shredded

4 whole cloves

1 cinnamon stick

2 tbsp brown sugar

2 tbsp balsamic vinegar

seeds of 1 pomegranate

fresh mint, to serve

Place the raisins in a bowl and pour over enough cold water to cover. Leave them to soak while you prepare the rest of the dish.

Heat a knob of the butter in a large heavy-based saucepan over a medium to high heat. Season the meat generously with salt and pepper. When the butter has melted and is bubbling, add the meat and brown. Do not overcrowd the pan. If necessary fry the lamb in batches. When nicely brown remove the meat to a plate and leave to one side.

Reduce the heat to medium before adding another knob of butter to the pan. Drop in the onions and cook gently for 8–10 minutes, by which time they should have turned golden and soft. Add the turmeric and fry, stirring for 1 minute. Tip in the flour and stir well to incorporate into the other ingredients. Fry for 1 minute.

Take the pan off the heat and pour in half the stock, stirring it in vigorously with a wooden spoon. Only when it is well incorporated should you pour in the remaining half and place the pan back over the heat. Increase the heat to maximum while stirring the hotpot. You are aiming for a velvety, thin gravy. Return the lamb to the pan and bring the mixture to the boil before turning the heat down to a simmer. Cover the pan and cook like this for about 1 hour.

Meanwhile, you can prepare the cabbage. Place the red cabbage, spices, sugar and vinegar in a saucepan and add a splash of water. Season generously with salt and pepper. Place over a medium to high heat. When the liquid is boiling give the whole lot a good stir, put a lid on the pan, reduce the temperature to minimum and leave to braise like this for about 20 minutes.

When the meat has cooked for an hour it should just be becoming tender and the gravy should have thickened well. If it hasn't, then continue to cook. If the mixture looks like it is becoming dry then just add a little water or stock as needed.

Preheat your oven to 180°C/gas 4.

When the meat is ready, drain the raisins and tip them in along with the Worcestershire sauce. Mix well. Pour the delicious meat and gravy into a baking dish.

Cut the bread slices into triangles and lightly butter one side. Arrange the bread over the top of the dish, butter side up, overlapping the triangles. I like to think they look a little like the rooftops from *Coronation Street*. Once the whole dish is covered with the buttered bread, place in your preheated oven and bake for about 30 minutes until the bread is golden and crisp.

When the braised red cabbage has turned soft, add the pomegranate seeds, place in a bowl and top with some fresh mint leaves – it goes deliciously with the hotpot.

Serve up your hotpot with a twist with some mint sauce and a little nod to Betty.

PESTO SUMMER STEW

Here's a casserole so light that it will sit nice and comfortably, thank you very much, on the dinner table on even the warmest of summer evenings. And I've livened the whole thing up by adding my Mixed Herb Pesto (see page 79), which can be added from frozen. Told you I was clever!

Serves 4

2 tbsp olive oil

3 rashers smoked streaky bacon, sliced into 1cm strips

20 Chantenay carrots

1 large leek, trimmed, washed and chopped into 1cm rounds

1 large glass of white wine

300ml chicken stock

4 large chicken breasts, skin removed and fat trimmed

100g frozen peas

5 cubes of frozen Mixed Herb Pesto (page 79) or 3 tbsp of the same pesto, fresh

salt and pepper

Heat the olive oil in a large sauté pan over a medium heat. Add the chopped bacon, carrots and leek to the pan. Fry the ingredients over the same heat until they begin to take on a little colour and start to soften. This should take 4–5 minutes.

Increase the temperature to maximum before pouring in the wine and letting it reduce by three-quarters. Pour in the chicken stock, bring the liquid to the boil and reduce to a simmer. Slip the chicken in and simmer gently for 8–10 minutes. Don't overcook as the chicken breasts can dry out easily.

Tumble in the peas and the pesto, and watch as the pesto melts into the stew, turning it an awesome green colour. Season with the salt and pepper. Simmer for another minute before serving up.

FREEZING -
BRRRRRR

Freezing: *adjective* below 0°C, very cold
verb store at a very low temperature as a means of preservation

Almost every fridge comes with one but if you're anything like me then your freezer has become the storage place for half-eaten tubs of ice cream, lone frozen peas and prehistoric pizzas.

Well, that was before I wised up, and now I find myself in that slightly smug position of always having a fitting frozen dish for any occasion stacked up and labelled neatly (OK, I'm lying about the neatness). As you know, I'm nowhere near perfect, and my bottle of vodka still holds pride of place, but have a read through this and you too may begin to realize that your freezer is more friend than foe.

Here are the top three major methods of freezing food, plus a little bit on how to freeze fruit. But there are a few basic rules to follow, such as:

- Make sure your freezer is in good working order. Finally tick it off your to-do list and defrost it.

- Label everything you put in, even if you think you will remember what it is. If you're like me you never will. Write down the date it was frozen, and try to use up within 4 months.

- Do not refreeze defrosted and reheated produce.

- Let cooked ingredients cool to at least room temperature before putting them in the freezer. It's better still if they are cold.

- Make sure everything you put in the freezer is covered or sealed, to avoid the build-up of ice crystals and freezer burn.

- When reheating, make sure you reheat to the very core. With bigger items, begin reheating covered at a low heat such as 160°C/gas 3 before uncovering and ramping the heat to around 190°C/gas 5.

- Ensure that you rotate your frozen produce, so that nothing festers in the frozen depths.

PIECE FREEZING

This is how I describe the process of freezing small individual dishes that you might want to defrost one by one. You will find super-handy ways to have things like nuggets for the kids, fancy fish cakes for an impromptu dinner for two, and some savoury scones to give to really annoying guests that turn up unexpectedly.

The best way to freeze the following dishes is to cook them and then let them cool to room temperature or below. Once they're totally cooled, put the items you want to freeze on a baking tray lined with baking parchment and place them flat into the freezer. Leave to cool for a minimum of 6 hours, by which point they should be frozen solid. It is now that you can take them from the baking tray and place the individual portions into resealable sandwich bags to save space.

The dishes in this section can all be reheated from frozen by following the instructions for each recipe.

A TASTE OF EASTERN PROMISE

Serve this at your next dinner party and I guarantee you will be handing out the recipe to everyone you serve it to! It has never failed to wow . . .

Serves 6

6 free-range egg yolks
150g caster sugar
250ml full-fat milk
250ml double cream
2 tsp vanilla extract
90g pistachios

Whisk the yolks with half the caster sugar in a large bowl until they are thick and creamy.

Pour the milk, cream and remaining caster sugar into a pan and bring up to the boil.

Pour the hot milk into the whisked yolks and sugar and give it a good stir. Then pour the mixture back into the pan and cook over a very low heat, stirring constantly with a spatula until the mixture is thick enough to coat the back of a spoon. Stir in the vanilla.

Let it cool for a bit then pop it into the fridge for an hour.

Pour into an ice-cream maker and churn until frozen, following the manufacturer's instructions. Now stir in the nuts. Line six little pots with clingfilm and spoon in the ice cream. Place them in the freezer and take them out 10 minutes before serving.

SPICED FISH CAKES

Fish cakes are the dish for every occasion, be it a solo supper or an intimate meal for two. I couldn't resist putting a little Middle Eastern twist on the old favourite by adding a dash of spicy harissa.

To reheat these fish cakes, place them on a baking tray and into an oven preheated to 180°C/gas 4, and bake for 35–40 minutes, until they are piping hot in the middle. If they begin to colour, then cover them with foil.

Makes 4 large fish cakes (or 6 small)

2 large, floury potatoes, peeled and roughly chopped into sixths

salt and pepper

2 bay leaves

200g sustainable white fish fillet, such as coley or ethical haddock, scaled but with skin on

200g salmon, scaled but with skin on

3 spring onions, trimmed and finely sliced

½ bunch of coriander, finely chopped

½ bunch of parsley, finely chopped

zest of 1 lemon

1 heaped tbsp harissa

2 tsp ground turmeric

80g plain flour

2 free-range eggs

150g fresh breadcrumbs

olive oil for frying

Put the potato chunks in a saucepan, toss in some salt, and cover with water. Place over a high heat, bring to the boil and cook for 8–10 minutes until tender. Drain the potatoes in a colander before returning them to the pan to steam dry from the residual heat.

Bring another saucepan, half filled with water, to just boiling, and add the bay leaves and plenty of salt. Place the white fish and the salmon in the water. Bring back up to just boiling, turn off the heat and leave the fish to sit in the warm water for 8 minutes, by which time it should be cooked through. Remove to a plate with a slotted spoon; discard the water and bay leaves. When the fish is cool enough to handle, use your fingers to remove the skin and flake large chunks of fish into a bowl.

Mash your cooked and dried potatoes. You don't have to make perfect mash; a few lumps won't affect the dish. Add the spring onions, coriander, parsley, lemon zest, harissa, turmeric and salt and pepper. Mix everything together. Drop in the fish chunks and, using a folding motion, incorporate the fish into the rest of the mixture. With clean hands, divide the mixture into four (or six smaller) balls, and squash each one lightly to form a fish-cake shape. Place on a plate lined with baking parchment.

Tip the flour into a bowl and season well with salt and pepper. Crack the eggs into another bowl and whisk with a fork. Drop the breadcrumbs into a third bowl and finally, to complete your breadcrumb production line, place a non-stick baking tray at the very end. Take one fish cake and drop into the flour, turning it over a couple of times to ensure it is well coated. Pick it up and place in the beaten egg. Again, ensure the fish cake is well covered with egg. Carefully move your fish cake from the egg into the breadcrumbs, and coat well. Place your crumbed fish cake on the baking tray and repeat with the remaining fish cakes.

Over a medium to high heat, heat up enough olive oil to cover the base of a large non-stick frying pan (about 0.5cm deep). When the oil is hot add the fish cakes. Fry for about 3 minutes on each side, or until the breadcrumbs have turned golden. When they are cooked, place them on clean kitchen paper to remove excess oil. Enjoy with some tartare sauce and salad, or cool completely and freeze as described on page 68.

CHICKEN AND FISH NUGGETS FOR THE KIDS

Kids love nuggets – fact. But you don't want to be giving them the over-processed, over-priced frozen version again and again. So why not make your own – and the good news is that they can be cooked from frozen just like the ones in packets. I have combined both fish and chicken into the same recipe, as apart from the main protein ingredient they are identical.

To reheat these nuggets from frozen, scatter them onto a non-stick baking tray and place in an oven preheated to 180°C/gas 4. Bake for 20 minutes, by which time they should be piping hot to the core.

Makes 18

350g trimmed chicken breast or 350g skinless and boneless sustainable white fish

100g plain flour

salt and pepper

2 free-range eggs

150g fresh white breadcrumbs (you can use wholegrain bread to be uber-healthy – the nuggets will end up a bit drier, and crunchier)

2–3 tbsp olive oil

Preheat your oven to 190°C/gas 5.

Slice the chicken or fish into strips that are about 2cm thick and about 5cm long. You don't have to keep exactly to the measurements, but try to keep the pieces roughly the same size to ensure they all cook in the same amount of time. Place your chicken or fish strips to one side.

Tip the flour into a wide but shallow bowl. Season well with salt and pepper. Crack the eggs into another wide but shallow bowl and whisk thoroughly. Tip the breadcrumbs into . . . you've guessed it, a wide but shallow bowl. Place these bowls in this order to form your production line. At the very end of the line place a flat non-stick baking tray. You are now ready to breadcrumb.

To avoid breadcrumbing your whole hand try to stick to this rule: one hand for the dry ingredients, and the other for the egg. With this rule in your mind take a piece of fish or chicken, one at a time, and drop into the flour. Roll around in the flour until well coated. Next drop into the beaten egg, and using the other hand coat the chicken or fish with the egg. Let any excess egg drip off before dropping into the breadcrumbs, using the dry hand to roll around to coat in the crumbs. Lastly, remove from the breadcrumbs and place onto your baking tray. Repeat the process with the remaining slices of chicken or fish.

Drizzle the olive oil all over the breadcrumbed chicken or fish before placing into your preheated oven. Bake the nuggets, turning once, for about 20 minutes, by which time they should have turned crisp and be fully cooked all the way through.

SAVOURY SCONES

Scones are a wonderful thing to have on standby in the freezer. They cook straight from frozen and are perfect to pull out when friends/neighbours/teenagers drop by unannounced. I've opted for savoury scones here, as I think they are great as a snack.

To reheat, place the frozen scones on a non-stick baking tray and bake in the oven at 180°C/gas 4 for 12 minutes, by which time they should be hot to the core.

Makes about 20

1 tbsp olive oil

8 rashers bacon, chopped into 1cm strips

500g strong white flour, plus a little extra for dusting

85g butter, cubed and cold

4g salt

5 tsp baking powder

80g strong Cheddar, grated

12 sun-dried tomatoes, drained and roughly chopped

4 free-range eggs

250ml milk

Preheat your oven to 210°C/gas 6.

Heat the olive oil in a frying pan over a medium to high heat. When hot, drop in the bacon strips and fry, stirring regularly, for about 2 minutes, by which time they will be cooked and have coloured. Tip the cooked bacon strips onto a piece of kitchen paper to drain excess fat. Leave to cool while you carry on with the rest of the recipe.

Tip the flour into a bowl and add the butter and salt. Using a rubbing action with your fingers, work the butter into the flour until you end up with a mixture that resembles breadcrumbs. Add the baking powder, bacon, Cheddar and the sun-dried tomatoes, and mix together roughly with a fork.

Crack 3 eggs into a jug and add the milk. Whisk together until you have a smooth mixture then pour this into the dry ingredients. Blend the wet and dry ingredients lightly with a fork until they start to come together.

Dust a clean surface with a little extra flour and tip the mixture onto it. Lightly bring together into a dough – do not knead the mixture. Using the palm of your hand, lightly push the dough until it is about 3cm thick – there is no need to be totally accurate here. Use an 8cm cutter to cut out your scones, and place them on a non-stick baking tray as you go. When you can't punch any more scones from your dough, rework it into a ball, flatten back out with your palm, and start cutting more scones. Repeat this process until all the dough is finished.

Crack the last egg into a bowl and whisk. Use the beaten egg to brush the top of the scones. Place the tray into your preheated oven and bake for 15 minutes, by which time the scones should have risen and be beautifully golden on top.

BATCH FREEZING

This method is for when you make a mother load of a dish to see you through that evening meal, and some other time. These are often the sorts of dishes when you need a bit of annoying kitchen equipment that has to be pulled out from dark shelves deep in the kitchen – huge stock pots, food processors, things that are a pain to wash and to handle, so you want to make the most of them when you have them out.

Before, I used to simply scoop up the remains of a meal, place them in a bag and freeze. However, I have become more canny, and have realized that although these are by and large family meals, we're not always together when we eat. There may be two of us, three of us, or just me on my own, and it always seemed a waste to defrost a whole batch worth. I have solved my portion dilemma by utilizing all the new fabulous supermarket products that are out there. So, you lovely lot, here are my new favourite freezer containers:

ICE-CUBE TRAYS. Perfect for tiny portions, such as for babies' meals. I've now also realized that you can freeze pesto, and the ice-cube tray is perfect for that too. The best way to use it is to cool whatever you are freezing to room temperature, fill an ice-cube tray with it, and freeze for at least 6 hours. When the cubes are totally frozen, pop them out and place them into a resealable bag, et voilà, cubes of food.

PLASTIC COFFEE CUPS. These are great for single portions of bolognaise, and are cheap and easy to throw away.

SANDWICH BAGS. There are some brilliant products out there that make it incredibly easy to 'pour and store' your meals. Investigate!

SPAGBOL FOR ALL

I do not apologize for the bluntness of this recipe, there is nothing clever or gimmicky about this dish, it does what it says on the tin. What I can say is that you should all be making this recipe once a month and freezing it in portions to satisfy almost any occasion. Freeze in ice-cube trays for young kids, in plastic cups for individual adult servings, and in a large zip-lock bag when you need a quick fix for friends coming over.

Serves (everybody) 6-8

4 tbsp olive oil

2 onions, diced

4 garlic cloves, finely chopped

2 large carrots, peeled and diced into 1cm cubes

4 celery sticks, diced into 1cm cubes

1kg minced beef

2 tbsp tomato purée

4 sprigs of thyme

2 bay leaves

1 large glass of red wine

2 x 400g tins chopped tomatoes

300ml beef stock (from a cube is fine)

Heat 2 tablespoons of the oil in a large flameproof casserole dish over a medium to high heat. When hot, add the onions, garlic, carrots and celery. Fry the vegetables, stirring regularly, for about 8–10 minutes, by which time they should have started to soften and lightly colour. Turn down the heat a little if you feel like you are losing control.

While the vegetables are frying, heat up 1 tablespoon of oil in a large heavy-based frying pan over a high heat. When the oil is hot, tip in half the minced beef and fry, stirring occasionally to break up any lumps, for about 3 minutes, by which time the mince should be cooked and browned in places. Spoon the cooked mince in with the frying vegetables. Pour in the remaining oil and again wait until it is hot before adding the remaining raw mince. Fry this batch of mince like the first, and again, when it is cooked, add to the pan with the vegetables along with any juices that have come from the meat.

Stir your meat and vegetables together and increase the heat to maximum. Stir in the tomato purée, along with the thyme and bay leaves (don't forget to remove these at the end!). Fry the mixture over a high heat for 1 minute before pouring in the red wine. Let the red wine reduce by half, then add the chopped tomatoes and stock. Bring the whole lot to a boil, before reducing the heat to a simmer. Cook like this for 45–60 minutes, stirring occasionally, by which time the meat should be very soft and the liquid reduced considerably. If during the cooking process you feel you need to add more liquid then simply pour in a little water and stir in.

Let the bolognaise cool completely before divvying up between containers to freeze.

BLACKBERRY SOUFFLÉ

What, the most delicate of dishes can handle the deepest, darkest recesses of the freezer? Yes, you can have a stunning soufflé on standby in the freezer and, what's more, if you follow the recipe then I promise it will work every time. Freeze this soufflé in its raw state, once you have spooned the mixture into the ramekins. Clingfilm tightly and freeze for at least 6 hours.

Makes 6 small soufflés

300g blackberries

160g caster sugar, plus 4 tbsp for dusting

2 heaped tbsp cornflour, mixed with ½ tbsp water

knob of butter

3 free-range egg whites

chopped pistachios and ginger nut biscuits, to serve

Place the blackberries, the 160g sugar and a splash of water in a saucepan over a medium heat. Let it come to a simmer and cook like this for about 5 minutes, until the blackberries have broken down and the sugar dissolved. Use a stick or jug blender to blitz the mixture to a purée, then push through a sieve into a clean pan to remove all the seeds.

Gently heat the purée over a low to medium heat, stirring regularly. When warm, add the cornflour and mix in thoroughly. Keep stirring the liquid over a low heat until it thickens. Pour the mixture into a clean bowl and leave to cool.

Use your finger to lightly grease the insides of the ramekins with the butter. Now spoon in a tablespoon of caster sugar and, by picking up the ramekin, work the sugar around the inside. It should stick to the butter, leaving a light dusting of sugar. Tip the excess sugar into the next ramekin and repeat the process until you have four ramekins lined with sugar and butter. Place the ramekins on a baking tray.

Preheat your oven to 190°C/gas 5 if eating straight away.

Pour the egg whites into a clean bowl and whisk with an electric hand whisk until they have doubled in size and become light and foamy. Sprinkle in the remaining 3 tablespoons of sugar and continue to whisk until the egg whites become a little thicker and glossy.

Drop a third of the whisked egg white mix into the fruit purée and work in with a metal spoon until smooth. Drop in the remaining egg white mix and fold, trying to conserve as much of the air as possible.

Divide the mixture equally between your ramekins, filling right to the top. Use a butter knife to smooth the top.

If you're freezing the soufflés, cover with clingfilm and place in the freezer now.

Place in your oven for 8–10 minutes, by which time the soufflés should have risen. Top with a few chopped pistachios and serve with ginger nut biscuits.

If cooking from frozen, cook for 12–14 minutes, using exactly the same oven temperature, and serve immediately.

MIXED HERB PESTO

Who would have thought that pesto, one of the freshest and most vibrant ingredients, could be frozen?! Well it can, and it means that by making one batch of the following recipe you will always have a burst of flavour on standby in your freezer.

Makes enough to fill a large ice-cube tray

1 small bunch of tarragon, roughly chopped

1 small bunch of basil, roughly chopped

1 bunch of chives, roughly chopped

1 small bunch of mint, roughly chopped

1 small bunch of parsley, roughly chopped

zest of 1 lemon

50g toasted pine nuts, plus a few extra for garnish

40g Parmesan, grated

about 100ml olive oil

Place all the ingredients into a food processor and blend until smooth. Season well.

Use immediately, or spoon the pesto into an ice-cube tray to be frozen.

TRAY FREEZING

This method uses the foil trays you can buy in almost every supermarket nowadays. There is nothing particularly fancy about these recipes, which is partly their point. They are ones you can turn to when your family is screaming out for something homely to converge around. These recipes are for those occasions when you've arrived home knackered and everybody wants something warming and satisfying, but you just don't have the time or energy to prepare from scratch.

To freeze these dishes, cook as per my recipe, and then let the dish cool completely to room temperature, or in the fridge. Cover tightly with clingfilm and then a layer of tin foil and freeze at least overnight. Once fully frozen, the meals can be stacked one upon another.

Each recipe comes with the reheating method, but just make sure that they are piping hot in the middle. If you are able to plan in advance, the following dishes reheat best after being fully defrosted.

COTTAGE PIE STANDBY

I don't know anybody who doesn't like cottage pie. It's like saying you don't like chocolate – it's impossible. So it makes sense to have one in the freezer on standby. Even though I've added a bit of spice and heat, this is a no-fuss recipe that will please all, from your children to your vicar.

To reheat from frozen, place the tray in an oven preheated to 170°C/gas 3 and bake for 35 minutes, then increase the heat to 190°C/gas 5 and cook for a further 15 minutes – by which time the pie should be hot to the core.

Serves 4–6

4 potatoes, peeled and chopped into sixths

salt and pepper

large knob of butter

splash of milk

2 tbsp olive oil

1 large onion, diced

3 carrots, grated

2 red chillies, deseeded and finely diced

2 tsp ground cumin

1kg minced beef

1 heaped tbsp plain flour

350ml beef stock (from a cube is absolutely fine)

250g frozen peas

75ml Worcestershire sauce

Place the potato pieces in a saucepan along with a good pinch of salt. Cover with water and bring to the boil. Simmer for about 10 minutes, by which time they should be tender. Drain in a colander. Drop your large knob of butter into the pan and pour in the milk. Over a low heat, melt the butter in the milk before tipping in the potatoes. Mash the potatoes together with the butter and milk until smooth. Leave to cool.

Heat the olive oil in a large flameproof casserole dish over a medium to high heat. When hot, add the onion and carrots. Fry for about 5 minutes, by which time they will have softened and taken on a little colour. Add the chillies and cumin and fry for a further minute, stirring constantly.

Increase the heat to maximum and drop in the mince. Fry for 3–4 minutes, breaking up the bits of meat with a wooden spoon. Spoon in the flour and mix in well with all of the juices. Continue to fry for 1 minute.

Pour in the beef stock, and bring the whole lot to a boil before reducing to a simmer. Cook like this for 15 minutes, by which time the liquid should have reduced and the sauce thickened a little. Stir in the peas, Worcestershire sauce and a generous amount of salt and pepper before taking off the heat.

Preheat the oven to 200°C/gas 6.

Tip your cottage pie filling into a foil tray or freezerproof baking dish (roughly 4cm deep x 15cm in diameter) – you'll need at least a couple of trays/dishes. Let the mixture cool down a little. Dollop on your buttery mash and use a spoon to smooth it out over the surface of the meat – try to make the top as smooth as possible. Take a fork and run it back and forth along the length of the potato topping. Do the same thing across the width so that small bits of potato become roughed up. Once the pie is baked these will turn crisp and golden.

Place the pie in the preheated oven and bake for 30 minutes, by which time the sides should be bubbling up and the top have turned golden brown. To freeze, follow the instructions on page 79.

NAN'S FISH PIE

Just the perfect dish to have lurking in your freezer. Imagine having the comforting warmth of a fish pie available to go in just 45 minutes. When I make this, I double up and do two, which makes the effort much more worthwhile. To reheat from frozen, place in an oven preheated to 170°C/gas 3 and cook for 35 minutes, after which time you should increase the temperature to 190°C/gas 5 and bake for a further 15 minutes.

Serves 4–6

4 potatoes, peeled and roughly chopped into sixths

salt

50g butter, plus a large knob

500ml milk, plus an extra splash

2 bay leaves

250g undyed smoked haddock

250g skinless haddock

1 leek, trimmed and chopped into thin rings

50g plain flour

50g Parmesan, grated

juice of 1 lemon

1 small bunch of parsley, finely chopped

12 large raw king prawns, peeled

3 free-range hard-boiled eggs, roughly chopped

Preheat the oven to 190°C/gas 5.

Place the chopped potato pieces in a saucepan along with a good pinch of salt. Cover with water and place over a high heat to bring to the boil. Simmer the potatoes for about 10 minutes, by which time they should be tender. Drain in a colander. Drop your large knob of butter into the still warm pan and pour in the splash of milk. Over a low heat, melt the butter in the milk before tipping in the boiled potatoes. Use a masher to mash the potatoes together with the butter and milk until you reach a smooth mash. Leave to cool while you cook the rest of the dish.

Pour the 500ml milk into a saucepan and add the bay leaves. Bring the milk to just below boiling and add both the smoked and unsmoked haddock. Bring the milk back up to a simmer before taking the pan off the heat. Leave the fish to sit in the hot milk for 10 minutes then remove the fish to a plate with a slotted spoon and leave to cool. Strain the milk through a sieve and keep to one side.

Heat the 50g butter in a large saucepan over a medium to high heat. Once melted and bubbling add the chopped leek. Fry the leek, stirring regularly, for 3–4 minutes, by which time it should have started to soften.

Add the flour to the mixture and stir vigorously to incorporate into the butter and leeks. Cook the mixture over a medium to high heat, stirring constantly, for 1 minute. Don't worry if it looks a bit like a mess at this point. Take the pan off the heat and pour in a third of the strained milk. Stir this in off the heat – again, the mix may look a little claggy,

but persevere. Pour in another third of the liquid and stir to mix in before replacing the pan over the heat and pouring in the remaining strained milk. Heat the mixture to boiling while stirring constantly. It should thicken up to a beautifully smooth sauce.

Remove the sauce from the heat and drop in the Parmesan, lemon juice and parsley. Again, mix to incorporate all of the ingredients.

Next, using your fingers, remove the skin from the smoked haddock and break up all the fish into large flakes. Place these straight into the bottom of your foil tray. Top the fish flakes with both the raw prawns and the chopped-up boiled egg. Pour the prepared sauce over the top of all the fish and, using a spoon, lightly mix all the ingredients so they are evenly spread.

Top the whole lot with your prepared mashed potato and place in the preheated oven for about 35 minutes, by which time the sauce should be bubbling over the sides.

To freeze, follow the instructions on page 79.

YUMMY CHOCCY LOAF CAKE

This a wonderful cake to have in the freezer and is lovely just eaten plain with a cup of tea. Or if you fancy something a little more posh simply slice and fill with cream and raspberries!

Serves 6–8

175g butter, softened

175g caster sugar

3 free-range eggs

140g self-raising flour

90g ground almonds

1 tsp baking powder

100ml milk

5 tbsp cocoa powder

2 tsp almond extract

60g chocolate (plain or milk), grated

Preheat the oven to 160°C/gas 3. Grease and line a 900g loaf tin with baking parchment.

Beat the butter and sugar with an electric whisk until light and fluffy. Then beat in the eggs, flour, almonds, baking powder, milk, cocoa and almond extract until smooth. Stir in the grated chocolate, then scrape into the tin.

Place in the preheated oven and bake for 1 hour then insert a skewer in the middle of the cake. If it comes out clean it's done, if not, cook for another 10 minutes.

Cool in the tin, then lift out onto a wire rack.

To freeze, put the cake in a polythene bag in a rigid plastic container. Defrost at room temperature.

FREEZING FRUIT

We all know and experience that feeling when all the fruit we bought from the supermarket with the best intentions of eating it starts growing a beard in the fruit bowl. Fruit seems to be one of those things we overbuy, and will therefore always throw away. Well, what if I told you that it can all be frozen and come into use at a later date in spectacular fashion? It won't be long before you become a converted frozen-fruit fanatic. Here are a few examples of how to freeze fruits, and what to do with them.

I haven't tried all fruits yet, but the following are some that I have, along with a use for them. Have a go – I haven't yet found much you can't freeze, although oranges were a bit of a disaster!

BERRIES

HOW: Scatter them on a tray lined with baking parchment. Place in the freezer and leave for a minimum of 6 hours before placing in a resealable bag.
USE: Carefully melt two large bars of white chocolate with about 100ml double cream in a saucepan over a low to medium heat. Tip your frozen berries into bowls, and allow your guests to pour the delicious hot chocolate sauce all over their frozen berries to make an unbelievably yummy, yet easy pud.

APPLES AND PEARS

HOW: Quarter, de-core and peel, before chopping in half again and freezing the chunks on a lined tray for 6 hours before placing in a resealable bag.
USE: Tip your frozen fruits into a saucepan, add a knob of butter, a scattering of brown sugar and a splash of water. Bring to the boil before pouring into a baking dish. Top with crumble mix made from rubbing together equal quantities of butter, sugar and flour, and a tiny touch of ground cinnamon until you reach a breadcrumb-like texture. Bake in the oven for 30 minutes.

PLUMS AND NECTARINES

HOW: De-stone, and chop into large chunks before placing on a lined tray and freezing for a minimum of 6 hours, then place in a resealable bag.

USE: Tip into a saucepan with a couple of dessertspoons of caster sugar and a splash of water. Bring to the boil, then take off the heat, leave to cool and mix in a splash of vanilla extract. Fold through whipped cream for a sunshine fruit fool.

PINEAPPLES

HOW: Peel, and chop into chunks before placing on a lined tray and freezing for 6 hours, then place in a resealable bag.

USE: If you have a powerful jug blender then frozen pineapple, rum, coconut water and lime juice make for a delicious cocktail.

BANANAS

HOW: Peel your bananas and insert a lollipop stick into each one. You can simply freeze them like this, but for a tasty alternative (that's a hit with the kids), you can add a chocolate twist. Melt some dark chocolate over a bain marie or in the microwave. Dip the bananas in the chocolate, coat in hundreds and thousands, and place on a lined baking tray to freeze. Pull out when feeling the heat in the summer for a homemade ice lolly.

LIMES AND LEMONS

HOW: Squeeze the juice from limes and lemons, keeping them separate. Pour the juice into ice-cube trays.

USE: You will never be without lemon or lime for your G&T or rum cocktail, for as the ice cube melts, it will slowly release the juice into your drink.

PERFECT PIZZA BASES

It is very nearly impossible to avoid frozen pizzas, which cook so conveniently from frozen and are tasty enough to please the hordes. So, if you can't beat them . . . make 'em fresh.

You cook these pizza bases in a frying pan, before cooling and freezing in between sheets of baking parchment. To make your pizza, you simply need to spoon some passata onto one of the frozen bases, throw on your favourite toppings, such as salami or olives, top the whole thing with grated Cheddar or mozzarella, and then bake in an oven preheated to 200°C/gas 6 for 10–15 minutes, by which time the base will be hot through and the cheese melted.

Makes 6 small, 3 medium bases

- 1 sachet (7g) dried active yeast
- 1 tbsp sugar
- 325ml warm water
- 500g strong white flour, plus a little more for dusting
- 2 tbsp olive oil, plus more for greasing and frying
- 5g salt

Add the yeast and sugar to the warm water. Stir the mixture vigorously until you are sure that both the sugar and the yeast are fully dissolved. Leave this mixture for about 5 minutes, by which time you should see little bubbles forming on the top of the liquid.

Tip the flour into a bowl and add the 2 tablespoons of olive oil and the salt. Pour in the yeast mixture and bring together, using a wooden spoon. When all the ingredients are reasonably well combined, tip the dough out onto a clean surface lightly dusted with flour.

Now's the time to work off those bingo wings – get your hands stuck in and knead the dough for at least 5 minutes, when it should have become smooth and elastic. Roll the dough up into a ball and place in a large clean bowl, lightly greased with olive oil. Cover with a clean tea towel or clingfilm and place in a warm area for 1½ hours, when the dough should have doubled in size.

Tip the dough onto a lightly floured surface and knead again until the air has been knocked out. Divide into three or six equal-sized balls and leave on a lightly floured surface in a warm place for 20 minutes to rise again.

When the dough has had its second rise, take each ball and roll out to make a circle about 13cm or 23cm in diameter, depending on the size of pizza you want.

Use enough oil to cover the base of a good, non-stick frying pan with a shallow layer, and place over a medium to high heat. When hot, carefully place the pizza bases, one by one, into the hot oil. Fry in the pan for 3–4 minutes on each side, before removing onto clean kitchen paper to remove any excess oil. When all the bases are cooked, leave them to cool separated by sheets of baking parchment.

Once cool, take each pizza base and wrap tightly in clingfilm and then tin foil before stacking in the freezer.

TOMATO SAUCE

This is a tomato sauce that pleases all and sundry. It's great just poured over boiled pasta, but also very good when thrown in from frozen with some fried mince to make a bolognaise. Because it contains vegetables and herbs, it packs enough punch to both fill you up and satisfy your taste buds. We get through gallons of this in my house, so when I make it, I go large. Feel free to halve this recipe if you don't have huge amounts of space in your freezer, or a ravenous family.

You can heat this sauce directly from frozen in a microwave or in a saucepan with a lid. If reheating in a microwave, ensure you stir the sauce and leave it to stand so it is heated evenly. Alternatively you can throw a block of this into a saucepan, drizzle in some water, place over a low to medium heat with a lid on, and leave to melt for 10 minutes. Stir occasionally, and once it has all melted increase the heat to boil the sauce for at least 2 minutes.

Serves the masses

3 tbsp olive oil

1 large red onion (or 2 small), finely diced

1 large carrot, peeled and finely diced

3 celery sticks, trimmed and finely diced

3 garlic cloves, finely chopped

2 bay leaves

1 bunch of basil, leaves only

2 x 400g tins chopped tomatoes

1 tbsp brown sugar (caster is fine if you don't have brown)

salt and pepper

Heat the olive oil in a large saucepan over a medium to high heat. When hot, add the onions and fry for 3 minutes. Add the carrot, celery and garlic, and continue to fry, stirring regularly, for a further 5 minutes, by which time all of the vegetables should have softened.

Drop in the bay leaves and half of the basil leaves, left whole. Increase the heat to maximum and continue to stir and fry for 1 minute.

Pour in the chopped tomatoes. Fill each tin halfway with water to swill out all the remnants of the tomatoes and add to the sauce. Drop in the sugar and stir. Bring the sauce to a simmer, and cook, stirring occasionally, for a minimum of 15 minutes, when it should have reduced and thickened.

Remove from the heat. Finely chop up the remaining basil leaves and add to the sauce along with a generous amount of both salt and pepper.

FROZEN WEDGES

We all love a chip every now and then; be it from the chip shop or from a frozen packet, they are the perfect accompaniment to breakfast, lunch and dinner. However, we all know that they are pretty bad for us – food can't be that delicious and not be bad for us. Or can it? I'm not saying the following wedges will make you live longer, but at least you can control the levels of fat and salt when you cook your own frozen wedges. I normally make double this recipe, eat half when they're ready and then freeze the rest.

To reheat, scatter your wedges onto a non-stick baking tray drizzled with a little olive oil, place in an oven preheated to 190°C/gas 5 and bake for 30 minutes, by which time the wedges should be piping all the way through.

Serves 4

**4 floury potatoes,
scrubbed clean**

salt

6 tbsp olive oil

Preheat your oven to 190°C/gas 5.

Take each potato in turn and chop into wedges, by slicing in half lengthways and then slicing each one of those halves into thirds lengthways on a slight angle to create the wedge shape.

Place the chopped wedges in a large saucepan and cover with water. Add a generous sprinkling of salt and place over a high heat to bring to the boil.

Pour the oil onto a heavy-based roasting tray and put the tray into the preheated oven while the potatoes are coming to the boil. It is important to have left your oil to heat in the oven for a minimum of 20 minutes.

Let the wedges simmer for 1 minute before draining them from the hot water. Toss the boiled wedges in the colander a few times. This is to release some of the steam, but also to rough up the edges of the potatoes. Leave the potatoes to cool a little in the colander.

When you are happy that the oil is hot, remove the tray from the oven and carefully scatter the drained potato wedges into the oil – take care, as the oil may spit. Replace the tray in the oven.

Roast your wedges for about 35–40 minutes, turning them two or three times to ensure even colouring.

To freeze your wedges, remove the cooked wedges from the tray and place onto a clean tray to cool to at least room temperature. When the wedges are cool, put them on a tray lined with baking parchment and place it, level, in your freezer for at least 6 hours. When they have frozen solid they can be scooped up and placed into resealable sandwich bags.

VEGETARIAN IN THE HOLE

Vegetarian: *noun* a person who does not eat or does not believe in eating meat, fish, fowl; *adjective* of or pertaining to vegetarianism or vegetarians

I have often written about how much I've struggled over the years with the vegetarians in my life – sisters, cousins, step-daughters, in-laws and Kaye Adams! At every stage of my life (as a cook) there's been someone who simply couldn't stomach (often quite literally) meat or fish of any kind. I've spurned vegetarian options, scoffed at vegetarian fine dining and generally been a pain when it comes to all things veggie-fied.

In my defence, I've had my reasons. Culturally, if you go to Jordan and say you're a vegetarian, they will look at you with extreme pity; they'll encourage you to sit down, take the weight off your feet, have a sip of water, take a deep breath and remain calm. In the Middle East, vegetarianism is an affliction, an illness.

So, as I write this introduction to my vegetarian section, it is with a measure of embarrassment that I must admit I never truly considered the fact that many vegetarians are in fact very serious AND considered in their decision not to eat meat.

For many years I viewed my vegetarian friends and relatives with culinary suspicion. You know what it's like. I thought their vegetarianism was an affectation. It was a way of being annoyingly different. They believed it was cool. Their cycling friends were doing it so they were doing it. They were force-feeding *The Good Life* on us all because they'd seen it on TV. As you can tell I had very little time for Veggies. I thought they were all moody glums!

Then a couple of years ago I realized I'd made an enormous mistake. It dawned on me that some of the people I have the funniest and most entertaining dining experiences with are in fact vegetarians! So, this is me admitting I was wrong! Admitting the problem was all my own! Admitting I should have been more tolerant! Admitting . . . That . . . Yes . . . OK . . . Veggie food can indeed be as good as . . . well – ordinary . . . proper . . . grown-up . . . food.

So, all my vegetarian friends and relatives, hear me! Finally, I admit it! I have embraced the word 'vegetarian'. But do NOT expect me to embrace the whole kit and caboodle. Vegetarianism is an entirely different prospect altogether – and every non-veggie on the planet knows exactly what I mean. The next time I (or any other non-veggie) admits they eat meat, please avoid the trademark responses of the -ism. You know what we carnivores mean: a pursing of the lips, a tightening of the eyes, a clenching of the jaw, a raised eyebrow and a look that kind of says, 'What is wrong with you, you savage mammal cannibal – you amoral serial killer of poultry? Repent! Repent!'

PS All the dishes below work brilliantly with a big fat juicy steak or lamb chop . . . and most of them will also sit very happily next to a roast chicken, leg of lamb or giant turkey – just saying!

VEGGIE SAUSAGE IN THE HOLE

This dish is for my dear friend Kaye Adams. She is the brightest, funniest, most accomplished woman I know. She also, I'm sad to say, suffers from an addiction . . . an addiction to Quorn sausages!

Serves 4

2 tbsp sunflower oil

8 Quorn sausages

3 red onions, sliced

250g plain flour

salt

4–6 sprigs of rosemary or thyme

150ml full-fat milk

150ml cold water

4 free-range eggs, whisked

Preheat the oven to 220°C/gas 7.

Once the oven is hot, put the oil in a large roasting tin, place it on a high shelf and leave for 10 minutes to heat up. Throw the sausages and onion into the hot roasting tin and return to the oven for 20 minutes.

Meanwhile, sift the flour into a large bowl with a good pinch of salt and add the herbs (remember to remove them before serving). Mix the milk in a jug with 150ml cold water. Make a well in the middle of the flour and add the eggs. Pour in a little milk and water, then whisk together to make a smooth batter. Mix in the rest of the milk and water mixture until the batter is the consistency of single cream. Leave it to rest at room temperature for 15 minutes.

Once the batter has rested, ladle it into the hot roasting tin (30cm x 25cm) – if it doesn't sizzle when you add the first spoonful, put the tin back into the oven until it does; this is vital for the Yorkshire to rise. Cook for 35–40 minutes. Do not even think about opening the door before the pudding is golden because, I promise you, it will flop! Serve straight away with mash, gravy and something green!

VEGETARIAN VINE LEAVES

My mum's veggie vine leaves are nothing like the insipid vile imitations of the real thing you get in little plastic packets (calm down, Nadia). These are absolutely delicious. I advise you to double the amount given here, as people always want more.

Serves 4–6, makes 40–50 vine leaves

1 aubergine

olive oil for frying

1 onion, diced

1 tsp tomato purée

100g basmati rice

100g paella or risotto rice

4 tbsp chopped walnuts

2 heaped tbsp chopped fresh mint

2 heaped tbsp chopped fresh dill

250g vine leaves (from a packet)

350ml tepid water

Cut the aubergine into 1cm cubes then toss in olive oil until lightly covered.

Cover the bottom of a frying pan with a thin layer of olive oil and fry the aubergine cubes on a medium heat, stirring all the time, until they begin to soften, then turn the heat up for a minute or two so that they brown slightly. Remove from the pan.

Put the onion in the pan and fry on a gentle heat until it begins to soften, then add the tomato purée. Stir-fry for about a minute then toss in all the rice. Stir on a very low heat until the rice is glistening – about a minute. Remove from the heat and add the walnuts and herbs, giving a good stir to make sure everything is well mixed.

If you are using vine leaves packed in brine you will need to rinse them a couple of times in cold water, swishing them around to remove some of the salt. Drain and taste to see if they are still too salty and, if so, rinse off in cold water. (There has to be some saltiness left as there is none in the fried mixture.) Do not use any that seem very tough and stringy. Remove any stems. Some of the vine leaves will be too big and tough to roll – set these aside and use them to line the bottom of the pan.

Lay a vine leaf out flat with the veined side uppermost and the stalk end (stalk removed) in front of you. Take a small handful of filling, squeeze slightly, then place on the nearest end of the vine leaf. Roll once, then turn in each side to make a parcel shape, and finish rolling to the end. A good finished size is about 6cm wide. Try to get them all the same size and thickness.

Lay some of the large unrolled leaves over the bottom of a saucepan about 21cm in diameter. Arrange the rolled vine leaves close together in the prepared pan. Add 350ml tepid water. Cover with a weighted plate and bring to the boil. Cover the saucepan and turn the heat down to a very low simmer. Cook for about 40–50 minutes, keeping an eye on the pan to make sure it doesn't dry out. After about 30 minutes remove the weighted plate and put the lid back on the pan. Continue cooking for about 15–20 minutes until you are sure that the rice is cooked (test one of the top ones).

BANGIN' BEETROOT BURGER

I cannot take the credit for this amazing beetroot beauty, that would be so wrong – although, believe me, I was sorely tempted! Nope, this beauty is the invention of my mate Rob Allison, damn fine gentleman and cook extraordinaire!

Ever since I devoured one of these babies at one of Rob's divine dinner do's it has become my go-to recipe whenever I have a new vegetarian to impress!

Makes 4 large or 6 smaller burgers

400g tin kidney beans, drained and rinsed

6 chestnut mushrooms

2 raw beetroot, peeled and grated

1 carrot, peeled and grated

1 red onion, roughly chopped into small pieces

50g smoked cheese, grated, plus extra for serving

½ bunch of parsley, roughly chopped

1 tsp ground cumin

½ tsp smoked paprika

4 tbsp olive oil

150g breadcrumbs

TO SERVE

burger buns

lettuce leaves

fresh tomato and tomato relish

toasted pine nuts

Place the drained kidney beans in a saucepan and cover them with water. Boil for 8 minutes before draining and cooling them. Then tip them into a food processor.

Add the mushrooms, beetroot, carrot, red onion, smoked cheese, parsley, cumin and paprika to the food processor. Blitz until everything is well mixed – a few chunks here and there is absolutely fine, in fact I quite like them.

Pour a tablespoon of the olive oil into a large frying pan over a medium to high heat. When the oil is hot, tip the mixture into the pan and fry it, stirring regularly, for about 10 minutes, by which time the mixture should be releasing quite a lot of liquid. Drain off the liquid and tip the fried vegetables into a bowl.

When the mixture has cooled to room temperature, tip in the breadcrumbs and mix the whole lot together – your hands are the best tools you have for this job, so don't be squeamish! It should all begin to clump together naturally. Divide the mixture into the number of burgers you want, and form patties using your hands. Shape isn't that important, but a uniform thickness is a great idea as it means your burger will cook through evenly.

Once you have made your patties, place them on a tray or plate lined with baking parchment. Put them in the fridge, uncovered, for at least 20 minutes, to help them firm up.

When you're ready to cook, heat a griddle pan (or frying pan if you don't have one) over a high heat. Remove your burgers from the fridge and brush lightly on both sides with the remaining olive oil. Carefully place the burgers on the pan and cook for 3–4 minutes on each side to ensure they are warm all the way through.

Toast the burger buns on the same pan – don't miss this bit out as it really makes a difference to the final taste. Construct your burgers, piling on lettuce, tomato, relish, extra smoked cheese and pine nuts. Feast greedily. Oh, yes please!

BEAN CHILLI

This recipe packs one hell of a punch. I have thrown the kitchen sink at it, and more. The flavour is smoky, dark and rich. You may notice a couple of odd-looking ingredients and think that I might have lost the plot (I wouldn't blame you), but, believe me, the addition of Marmite and cocoa powder take this chilli to a place even the most ardent meat-eaters will be impressed by. Promise! (I love a sausage or two with this!)

Serves 4–6

2 tbsp olive oil

1 carrot, peeled and finely diced

3 celery sticks, trimmed and finely diced

1 red pepper, trimmed and finely diced

2 sprigs of thyme

2 tsp ground cumin

1 tsp ground coriander

1 tsp smoked paprika

1 tsp ground cinnamon

2 tbsp Marmite

200ml vegetable stock

2 x 400g tins chopped tomatoes

salt and pepper

2 x 400g tins kidney beans, drained and rinsed

400g tin cannellini beans, drained and rinsed

1 tbsp cocoa powder

Heat the oil in a large saucepan over a medium to high heat. When hot add the carrot, celery and red pepper. Fry these ingredients for 5 minutes, stirring regularly. Add the thyme, cumin, coriander, paprika, cinnamon and Marmite. The mix will clag up a little, but continue to stir and fry for 1 minute before pouring in the stock and the chopped tomatoes.

Bring the mix to the boil before reducing to a simmer and cooking for 10 minutes.

Season generously with salt and pepper before adding all the beans to the mix. Bring back to a simmer and cook, stirring regularly, for a further 10 minutes. Sprinkle over the cocoa powder and stir in. Bring back to a simmer, check the seasoning and remove the thyme sprigs.

Serve up with chunks of crusty bread.

WHOLE PUMPKIN ROAST

I knew that this chapter needed a vegetarian alternative to a Sunday roast, but I was determined not to simply cobble together a nut roast, although I was tempted. Instead, I went to the supermarket and picked up a load of vegetables and ingredients that I thought I would like to eat. For a while I stared at the bulgur wheat, pumpkin, herbs and cheese, wondering how the hell I could tie the whole lot together. Then it hit me – chuck it all in the pumpkin and bake that.

There is method to my madness. I wanted to create a centrepiece, like a joint of meat, something to bring to the table to excited gasps, and that's how my pumpkin roast was born.

Scraping out the pumpkin flesh can take a bit of time, but is quite good fun – pretend it's Halloween. And don't throw those trimmings away: you can use them to make a delicious soup.

I suggest serving this not with traditional roast accompaniments but with fresh salads. I've come to the conclusion that there's no point trying to imitate a roast dinner, so instead celebrate everything that is great about veggies, and eat fresh and light for a Sunday change . . . well, maybe some roasties could work?

Serves 4–6

1 large pumpkin (I used a 2.2kg pumpkin, a size widely available in supermarkets)

4 sprigs of thyme, leaves only

4 sage leaves, very finely sliced

salt and pepper

4 tbsp olive oil

1 red onion, finely diced

2 garlic cloves, finely chopped

200g bulgur wheat

300ml vegetable stock

400g tin chopped tomatoes

½ bunch of parsley, finely chopped

1 aubergine, trimmed and sliced into thin (3mm) rounds

1 courgette, trimmed and sliced into thin (3mm) rounds

50g ricotta

80g feta

1 ball of mozzarella, drained

a few chopped walnuts

Preheat the oven to 160°C/gas 3.

Use a bread knife to slice the top off your pumpkin. You can afford to make this a reasonably thick slice, as it helps open up the mouth of the pumpkin. To keep it stable, take a very thin slice from the bottom of the pumpkin as well. Using a combination of a small sharp knife and a spoon, remove all the seeds from inside the pumpkin, and chuck them. Scrape the flesh until the walls are about 2–3cm thick. When you are satisfied with your pumpkin carving, place the hollow pumpkin on a baking tray.

Mix together the thyme and sage with a good amount of salt and pepper. Sprinkle the inside of your pumpkin with the herby seasoning. Put the pumpkin, along with its lid (but not on top), into the preheated oven and bake for 40 minutes, by which time it should be softening but still holding its shape.

In the meantime, heat up a tablespoon of olive oil in a large saucepan over a medium to high heat. When hot, add the onion and garlic and fry for about 3 minutes, stirring regularly. Add the bulgur wheat and stir to mix in. Pour in the stock and the chopped tomatoes. Season, and stir the mixture as it comes to a boil. Reduce the heat to a simmer, cover with baking parchment and leave to cook without stirring for 12–15 minutes, by which time the bulgur wheat will have expanded and soaked up the stock. Throw in the chopped parsley and mix in with a fork.

Heat some of the remaining olive oil in a large frying pan over a high heat. Season the aubergine and courgette slices with salt and pepper. When the oil is hot, add some of the slices in a single layer. Fry for about 1–2 minutes per side, before removing onto clean kitchen paper to remove excess oil. Repeat the process with the remaining aubergine and courgette slices.

Increase the temperature of your oven to 180°C/gas 4. Now we are ready to construct: lights–camera–action!

Remove the cooked pumpkin from the oven. Spoon in a quarter of your bulgur wheat mix, making sure you pack it down with a spoon. Use a teaspoon to drop some blobs of ricotta on top of the bulgur wheat. Crumble over a quarter of the feta. Cover with a quarter of the aubergine and courgette slices. Tear off a few pieces of mozzarella and place on top of the aubergine layer along with some of the chopped walnuts. Repeat this process a further three times, ensuring you pack the layers tightly as you go. The amounts should fill the pumpkin almost perfectly.

Place the lid on the pumpkin. Put the whole pumpkin in the oven and bake for 30 minutes. Once the pumpkin has cooked, let it sit for 5 minutes to allow any excess liquid to soak back into the bulgur wheat. Take it to the table to show off and then spoon out the delicious filling, wow-ing your guests all over again with how wonderful it tastes as well as looks!

PERSIAN PILAF

When vegetarian food tastes this good, you'll soon forget about meat! Although . . . this does go incredibly well with a slab of BBQ lamb . . . or pork . . . Oh, and chicken – sorry, I can't help myself.

Serves 4–6

½ large butternut squash, peeled and chopped into 2cm cubes

2 large red onions, 1 cut into 8 wedges and the other diced

4 tbsp olive oil

salt and pepper

knob of butter

2 garlic cloves, finely chopped

200g runner beans, cut at an angle into 2cm slices

1 bay leaf

2 tsp ground cumin

2 tbsp tomato purée

250g basmati rice, rinsed under cold running water

500ml vegetable stock

100g feta

½ bunch of parsley, chopped

1 bunch of dill, chopped

1 bunch of mint, leaves only, chopped

seeds of 1 pomegranate (totally optional)

Preheat your oven to 200°C/gas 6.

Scatter the butternut squash pieces and the onion wedges onto a baking tray, and drizzle over half the olive oil. Season with salt and pepper and place in the oven. Roast the vegetables for 20–25 minutes, turning once.

In the meantime, heat up the remaining olive oil and the knob of butter in an ovenproof high-sided frying pan over a medium to high heat. When hot, add the diced onion and chopped garlic. Fry, stirring regularly, for about 3 minutes, by which time the onion should have started to soften.

Tumble in the runner beans and the bay leaf, and continue to stir and fry for a further 2 minutes before spooning in the ground cumin and tomato purée. Keep frying for another minute, stirring regularly. The rice goes in next, and needs to be stirred through the rest of the ingredients.

Reduce the temperature of your oven to 180°C/gas 4.

Pour the stock into the frying pan and stir gently. Bring the liquid to the boil. Cover the pan with a piece of baking parchment cut to fit snugly over the top. Place the covered pan in the oven (move the tray of butternut squash to a lower shelf) and leave to bake for 15–20 minutes, by which time the stock should have been absorbed and the rice cooked to tender. Carefully remove the pan from the oven and let it sit for a couple of minutes.

Remove the baking parchment and spoon the rice onto a warm serving dish, fluffing it up as you go.

Arrange the roasted butternut squash and onion pieces on top of the rice before crumbling over the feta, scattering with herbs, then finishing with final flurry of pomegranate seeds (if using).

AMERICAN MAC 'N' CHEESE

I'm going to be honest here – I have in the past mucked about with the Great Macaroni Cheese! You know the sort of thing, a little chopped bacon here (sorry, guys, I know that's the hardest to give up!), some fried onions there. Delish, but this recipe is in honour of the great Mac 'n' Cheese that I always indulge in when I'm in New York! How flash! Yes, just good old-fashioned macaroni (no penne, please) and plenty of creamy cheese sauce is all that is needed for a trip to heaven.

Serves 4

400g macaroni

salt and pepper

70g butter

50g plain flour

900ml full-fat milk

100g strong mature Cheddar

FOR THE TOPPING

50g strong Cheddar, grated

1 tbsp Parmesan, grated

Cook the macaroni in plenty of salted boiling water until it is tender.

Meanwhile, melt 50g of the butter in a non-stick saucepan and whisk in the flour. Cook, stirring, for a couple of minutes, then gradually whisk in the milk until you get a smooth sauce. Cook, while stirring, for a few minutes until it thickens and then stir in your Cheddar until smooth. Take off the heat and season to taste. I like a fair bit of black pepper, but that's up to you.

Heat the grill up while you drain the macaroni. Rinse it (this will help the macaroni stay separate) under cold running water.

Pour the cheese sauce over the cooked pasta and put it into your baking dish. Top with the Cheddar and Parmesan and then dot with the remaining butter. Grill for 8–10 minutes or until brown and bubbling. Now, pleeeeease serve with a tomato salad, because it goes sooooo well!

ROASTED VEG ON PITTA AND HUMMUS

I am so excited about this dish: not only does it look beautiful, it's also supremely healthy and utterly delicious! And it's a bonus if there are any leftovers, because it all tastes just as good the next day! Hip hip hooray!

Serves 4

2 aubergines, cut into 2cm chunks

2 red onions, quartered

20 cherry tomatoes

1 or 2 red or orange peppers, deseeded and cut into 2.5cm chunks

3 or 4 garlic cloves, crushed

2 tbsp zaatar

a couple of glugs of olive oil

salt

4 round pitta breads

4 tbsp hummus

chopped fresh parsley, to garnish

Preheat the oven to 200°C/gas 6.

Mix the vegetables with the garlic, zaatar and olive oil (be generous with the oil!) in a roasting tin and spread out so that the veg is in a single layer – you might have to use two trays, because if there isn't enough room the veg will sweat rather than roast. Yuk! Season with a generous flourish of salt and put into the oven. I usually give the veg a bit of a shake or turn over every 10 minutes or so. After about 40 minutes, have a little taste. The aubergine will take the longest.

Warm the pitta bread, then spread with the hummus and top with the vegetables. Sprinkle with the chopped parsley. Wow, want some now!

RICH FENNEL AND TOMATO BAKE

I implore you to try this dish (even if you think it looks a bit weird). It is divine, either playing the starring role alongside a jacket potato and a big salad or happily sat next to a juicy pork chop!

Serves 4

2 large bulbs of fennel

1–2 tbsp olive oil, plus extra for coating

1 onion, sliced

1 large garlic clove, finely chopped

1 tsp fennel seeds

400g tin chopped tomatoes

salt and black pepper

FOR THE GREMOLATA

50g fresh breadcrumbs

50g grated fresh Parmesan (please, not dried – we all know what that tastes like!)

zest of 1 unwaxed lemon

2 cloves garlic, very finely chopped

Preheat the oven to 180°C/gas 4.

Trim the tops of the fennel bulbs. Slice the bulbs about 0.5cm thick. Toss the slices in olive oil until they are well coated then spread over an oven tray and bake in the oven for about 15 minutes until they begin to soften.

Pour 1–2 tablespoons olive oil into an ovenproof pan and sauté the onion and garlic for 3 or 4 minutes, then add the fennel seeds and stir-fry for about 30 seconds until they start to jump – but be careful they don't burn. Add the baked fennel, then pour in the tomatoes and season with salt and black pepper.

Bring to a simmer then remove from the heat. Mix together the gremolata ingredients and sprinkle over the top of the fennel mixture. Bake in a hot oven until the topping is golden.

SPICED ROASTED BABY BEETS AND CARROTS WITH HORSERADISH SAUCE

Beetroot and horseradish are a match made in heaven but unfortunately my kids don't agree as they 'HAAATE' beetroot . . . oh well, all the more for me!

Serves 4

800g mixed raw baby beetroots

400g carrots (baby ones would be nice)

2 tbsp brown sugar

1 tbsp cumin seeds

8–10 garlic cloves, unpeeled

olive oil

2 x 400g tins chickpeas, drained and rinsed

100g mixed salad leaves

200g Greek yogurt

2 tbsp creamed horseradish

Preheat the oven to 200°C/gas 6.

Peel and trim your baby beets and slice them in half. Leave the baby carrots whole, but halve the large ones lengthways. Place them on a large baking tray with the beets.

Mix together the sugar, cumin seeds, garlic cloves and a couple of glugs of olive oil. Then pour the mixture over the beets and carrots, making sure they are well covered. I usually give them all a good rub to be certain. Pop into the oven to roast for about 10 minutes, then add the chickpeas and cook until golden, about another 20–25 minutes.

To serve, scatter the salad leaves onto a large plate then top with the roasted beets, carrots, garlic and chickpeas. Mix together the yogurt and horseradish, adding more horseradish if it tastes like it needs it! Serve on the side.

SHARING
FOOD

Sharing: *verb* to divide and serve out in (sometimes) equal portions

SHARING FOOD!

A truly selfless act. Something I've always been a fan of. I like to think that the very concept of sharing has been almost hard-wired into my DNA due to my dear old dad's Bedouin roots. From time immemorial the Bedouins have been inviting complete strangers into their tents and homes to share in stories and food!

When I think of my ancestors welcoming thirsty, hungry, travelling tribes into their tents it reminds me of how I am almost compelled to drag everyone who walks through (or even, on occasion, past) my front door into my kitchen, where I immediately start clashing my pots and pans about! I am simply driven to share my cooking, and therefore my food, with others. For instance, if we ever have an unexpected visitor, in spite of my husband, Mark, protesting that I shouldn't worry, I literally cannot stomach the thought of not feeding them. I'd rather die than not share some kind of a feast! It's in my blood.

When most people think of sharing, they think of sharing what's on their plate with others, sharing their dessert (but not too much!) or their bag of chips. But for me sharing is much more than this. You see, if I'm cooking for you or my loved ones I'm effectively sharing time, company, stories, laughter and sometimes (not too often!) even tears. For me, sharing is truly caring.

My idea of heaven would be an ever-expanding dining table around which more and more friends and family sit. I'm never frightened by the number of mouths I need to feed, I'm only ever frightened that I might not have enough for me (there is no worse sin!)

And yet I've only recently realized that there is, in fact, a negative side to this sharing obsession of mine! Mark (who is English through and through) often says how wonderfully exotic my style of cooking and dining really is. Having grown up not even eating at a table, he says he adores the way cooking in our house is like staging a mini theatrical performance. But – he admits – there is one small element of this sharing impulse of mine that does slightly get on his nerves. Whenever we eat at home, out at a restaurant or at a friend's house, he says I just don't seem to see any boundaries between plates. Apparently my 'problem' is that whenever I spot something I like the look of on someone else's plate, I can't help but have a nibble, even if the person whose plate it's on is NOT a sharer! Mark and the girls say it can be very 'embarrassing' but I don't agree! I think it just shows that I am a sharer through and through. Well, we can't help our genes, can we?

So if, like me, you're a BIG sharer when it comes to cooking *and* eating other people's food, just get all your friends over and cook them some of these delicious recipes, then you can enjoy not only your own plate of gorgeous food but some of theirs too!

RISOTTO-STUFFED SALMON

I have blatantly stolen my husband's Nanny Thelma and made her MY Nanny Thelma! She is ninety-one years old and the brightest, funniest, toughest bird I know, and I love her very much . . . but she is a nightmare when it comes to food! Very fussy – but she loves this risotto-stuffed salmon and I love to cook it for her. Try this on the ones you love!

Serves 6

1 tbsp olive oil

large knob of butter

1 large leek, trimmed and finely sliced

2 garlic cloves, finely chopped

200g risotto rice

1 small glass of white wine

700ml warm vegetable stock (a cube is fine)

40g Parmesan, grated

50g mascarpone

juice of ½ lemon

3 tbsp finely chopped fresh chives

3 tbsp finely chopped fresh parsley

4 tbsp finely chopped fresh dill

salt and pepper

2 large salmon fillets (about 900g each), cut from the middle, scaled, bones removed and the belly trimmed

Heat the olive oil and butter in a saucepan over a medium to high heat. When the butter has melted and is bubbling lightly in the oil, add the chopped leek and garlic and fry for 4–5 minutes, by which time the vegetables will have softened. Add the rice and fry for 1 minute, stirring almost constantly. It is important that the rice is well covered in the oil and that it has this frying time.

Increase the heat to maximum and pour in the white wine. Let it bubble away until it has reduced by about two-thirds. Pour in about a quarter of the stock and start stirring. As the stock comes to the boil it will start to be absorbed by the rice. Add more stock when you feel that the rice is beginning to dry out. Continue stirring to unlock the creamy starch from the rice; the more stirring, the creamier the risotto. Continue the process of adding the stock gradually and then stirring until all the stock is used and the rice is cooked through. The consistency should be loose but creamy.

Reduce the heat to minimum and add both the Parmesan and the mascarpone. Stir the cheeses in until they are totally incorporated. Add the lemon juice, chives, parsley and dill, along with a generous amount of salt and pepper. Stir well to combine all the ingredients. Leave your risotto to one side. It is very important that it cools to at least room temperature.

When the risotto is cool, lay the salmon fillets in front of you skin side down. Season the flesh with salt and pepper. Begin spreading the risotto onto one of the salmon fillets. Cover the flesh all the way to the edges. You will find that the fillet has a natural unevenness to it; add more risotto where needed to create an even top. When you are satisfied with your covering, carefully pick up the other piece of salmon and lower it on top of the risotto-covered fillet to create a huge salmon sandwich.

Preheat your oven to 190°C/gas 5.

I like to tie my fish up. This helps with presentation, portioning and also moving the cooked fish later. But you don't have to do this. While preparing and tying, some of the risotto may seep from the sides – either scoop this up and try to force it back in or take it as a chef's perk.

Carefully place the fish on a baking tray lined with baking parchment and bake in the oven for 45 minutes, by which time it will be fully cooked through. Let the fish rest for 5 minutes before bringing to the table.

Serves 6

2 tbsp olive oil

6 skinless chicken breasts

salt and pepper

1 onion, finely diced

1 large red pepper, trimmed and chopped into 1cm cubes

1 courgette, trimmed and chopped into 1cm cubes

1 tsp ground turmeric

1 tsp ground cumin

1 tsp ground cinnamon

250–300ml chicken stock

3 preserved lemons, quartered – more if you like them

18 green olives, pitted

2.4 litres water

300g quick-cook polenta

90g Parmesan, grated

bunch of parsley, roughly chopped

CHICKEN WITH GREEN OLIVES AND PRESERVED LEMONS ON POLENTA

Not the most catchy title, I know! Preserved lemons can divide people, some love 'em, some hate 'em. I am a lover, and think they work perfectly with green olives.

Even if you don't like preserved lemons, take the polenta serving suggestion from this recipe and put it together with one of your favourite stews. The polenta acts as a dam for all of the juices from the stew, which means you can serve the whole dish up on a huge platter – a perfect sharing stew.

Heat the olive oil in a large flameproof casserole dish over a medium to high heat. Season the chicken breasts with salt and pepper and when the oil is hot lower into the pan. Fry on both sides for 2–3 minutes until the flesh has turned golden brown. Remove the chicken breasts from the hot oil and reduce the temperature to medium.

Add the chopped onions and fry, stirring regularly, for 4 minutes before adding the red pepper and courgette. Continue frying all of the vegetables together for a further 3 minutes, by which time they should have started to soften.

With the pan still over a medium heat, sprinkle in the spices and stir to combine with all of the vegetables. Fry for 45 seconds, stirring almost constantly so the spices don't burn. Pour in 250ml of the chicken stock and stir the ingredients into the liquid. Add the preserved lemons and the green olives. Stir while bringing up to a boil.

Place the browned chicken breasts back in the pan, pushing them down in the stock. You are aiming for the stock to come three-quarters of the way up the sides of the chicken; use more stock if necessary. Continue to cook for 15 minutes, or until you are satisfied that the chicken is cooked all the way through.

Meanwhile, bring 2.4 litres water up to the boil in a large saucepan. Once boiling, gradually pour in the polenta, whisking all the time. It should thicken up almost immediately, at which point you should switch tools to a wooden spoon and reduce the heat to medium-low. Beat the polenta over the heat for about 4 minutes, by which time it should be cooked through. Add the Parmesan, along with a generous amount of salt and pepper, and continue to beat until you are satisfied that the cheese has melted in fully.

To serve, spoon your polenta onto a large serving dish and push out to the sides, to create a dip. Spoon the chicken and sauce into the middle and marvel at how the polenta keeps the liquid from running everywhere, before adding your final flourish of chopped parsley.

NB You may notice that the amount of water I have suggested is about double the amount stated on the side of the packet. Do not fear, I haven't gone mad; these measurements create a loose-style polenta, which I prefer.

SLOW-COOKED PORK SHOULDER

Here's a recipe that's perfect for a girls' night of gossiping and Prosecco or a huddle of boys watching sport. There is a long cooking time, but it is well worth the wait, and once you've put the pork on, you hardly have to do anything to it. Mmm, more wine time!

Serves 6

2kg pork shoulder, boned weight

1 litre orange juice (bits in, bits out, doesn't matter)

3 sprigs of rosemary

3 sprigs of thyme

100ml tomato ketchup

40ml Worcestershire sauce

½ tsp smoked paprika, more if you like it hot

40g soft brown sugar

TO SERVE

toasted pitta breads

finely shredded red cabbage

sliced tomatoes

Place the pork shoulder into a large pot and pour over the orange juice. Add enough water to totally submerge the shoulder. Throw in the sprigs of rosemary and thyme.

Place the pot over a medium to high heat, and wait for it to come, just, to a boil. It is very important that the shoulder is not boiled; instead, at this point, reduce the temperature so that the liquid is only 'burping' – this means that the water is just under a boil. If the liquid boils it will dry the meat out. This may take a little adjusting, but is the most essential part of this recipe. Cook the pork like this for 4 hours. You can pretty much leave it to potter away in the background. The only thing to watch is if the liquid reduces to a level which means the meat is in contact with the base of the saucepan.

When the pork has had its cooking time, leave it to cool a little in the liquid, at least 20 minutes.

Put the tomato ketchup, Worcestershire sauce, smoked paprika and brown sugar in a bowl and whisk together until smooth. Divide the mixture in two at this point: half to glaze the pork and half to be placed on the table to serve.

Preheat your oven to 220°C/gas 7. Line a baking tray with some tin foil and then baking parchment. This is to protect your baking tray – you'll thank me later.

Remove the pork from the cooking liquid, roughly pat dry, and place onto your prepared baking tray. Cut off any really thick pieces of fat and then smother the shoulder in the sauce. Place the meat in the oven and roast for 30 minutes.

Keep checking your pork during the roasting time as, often, ovens can be hotter in certain spots, so if you see the meat burning in some places, turn it round a couple of times.

After 30 minutes of roasting, take the meat out and place on a chopping board. Either slice or tear the pork into chunks. To serve, fill toasted pittas full of the remaining pork, sauce, red cabbage and tomatoes.

POTATO BOULANGÈRE WITH LEG OF LAMB

This dish may well send you to an early grave. But with every mouthful of this gloriously unctuous meat and potato combo you will become more at ease with your early demise. You could pair this dish with some lovely steamed broccoli and kale, which I hear absolves all sin.

Serves 6–8

5 potatoes (Desiree or King Edward work perfectly), peeled

1 large onion, very finely sliced

a few sprigs of thyme

a few knobs of butter (optional)

1 medium leg of lamb

3 garlic cloves, finely sliced into batons

a few small sprigs of rosemary

salt and pepper

500ml hot chicken stock

Preheat the oven to 220°C/gas 7.

You need to slice your potatoes into the thinnest discs possible. This is best done on a mandolin (otherwise it's a right pain!), however I know not everybody will have one, so the best alternative is the sharpest knife you have. There is a little trick to help slicing: take a very thin slice from one side of the potato and place the potato on that sliced side on your chopping board. Because of the flat surface, the potato will sit far more steady as you go about trying to slice discs about 2–3mm thick.

Place about a third of your potato slices into the base of a baking dish or roasting tray at least 35cm x 20cm. It is not necessary to line the potatoes up, but try to arrange the slices so they are roughly the same depth all over the base. Sprinkle over about half the onion slices along with half the thyme sprigs and a few knobs of butter (if using). Cover with the second third of the potato slices, roughly evening them out again. Place the remaining onion slices, thyme sprigs and butter over the potatoes. Finish with the final potatoes. If you are going to make a neat layer, the final one is the one to put some effort into. Leave this to one side whilst you get on with your lamb.

Using a small sharp knife stab the leg of lamb in about 10 different places to create small pockets. Into each pocket stuff pieces of garlic and sprigs of rosemary. Season the lamb all over with lots of salt and pepper then place directly on top of the potatoes. Pour the hot stock slowly over the potatoes – it should come about three-quarters of the way up.

Place the dish in the oven and cook at the high heat for 25 minutes.

Remove from the oven and reduce the temperature to 170°C/gas 3. Cover the whole dish with tin foil and return to the oven. Roast for 1 hour, by which time the potatoes should be tender and the lamb totally cooked through. Remove the lamb and wrap tightly in tin foil to rest. Increase the temperature of the oven to 200°C/gas 6 and place the potatoes back in. Roast the potatoes for 15 minutes, by which time they will be deliciously browned on top and the lamb will have had time to rest.

To serve, unwrap the lamb from the foil and place back on top of the potatoes before triumphantly plonking into the middle of your dinner table to gasps of hungry excitement.

KOREAN BEEF

This wonderful recipe for Korean bulgogi was given to me by Yung He, a truly fabulous cook (and mum to my mate Rob), so hands together everyone – a round of applause, not to mention hip hip hoorays, are due.

Serves 6

900g rump steak, trimmed of fat and sliced into 1cm thick slices

6 tbsp light soy sauce

1 tbsp sesame oil

5 spring onions, trimmed and finely sliced

3 garlic cloves, finely chopped

1 tsp caster sugar

2–3 tbsp olive oil

TO SERVE

800g cooked sticky rice

rose harissa – kimchi is traditional, but I couldn't resist the Middle Eastern touch

baby gem lettuce leaves

1 finely sliced red chilli

Place the strips of rump steak in a bowl. Pour in the soy sauce and sesame oil and massage into the meat, using your hands. Drop in the spring onions, garlic and caster sugar, and again mix well. Leave this to marinate for a minimum of 4 hours but preferably overnight.

When ready to serve, heat up a large non-stick frying pan over a high heat. It will probably be necessary to cook the beef in two batches, unless you have a massive pan, so heat up half the oil in the pan. When the oil is smoking, add half the beef and fry, stirring occasionally, for 3–4 minutes, until the meat is just cooked. Tip the cooked meat into a serving dish, and repeat the cooking process with the remaining beef.

Encourage people to wrap up a bit of rice with a slice of beef, some chilli and a splodge of harissa in a lettuce leaf, and then eat it up in one.

PERFECT PAELLA

Come on, let's take the family to Spain for a lovely Sunday lunch . . . oh, OK then, let's do it here, it will be just as delish!

Don't be tempted to use chicken breasts as they'll dry out cooked this way. Chicken thighs are much more tasty.

Serves 6

6–8 tbsp olive oil

6 chicken thighs (non-meat-eaters can leave this bit out)

8 garlic cloves, quartered

2 large onions, thinly sliced

2 tbsp smoked paprika

1 red chilli, chopped (seeds removed if you don't like it hot)

4 large tomatoes, deseeded and skinned (or 400g tin chopped tomatoes)

1 large glass of wine

500g paella (or risotto) rice

1.5 litres hot chicken or fish stock

15 strands of saffron (optional)

salt and pepper

1kg whatever shellfish you fancy (I like mussels, clams, prawns)

3 squid, cleaned and sliced

small bunch of parsley, chopped

2 lemons, quartered

I use a 45cm paella dish, but you can use a large frying pan. I also use a special paella outdoor gas ring that I bought online for thirty quid, but you can use two rings on your hob – although it's hard to cook it evenly!

Heat the oil in the paella pan until very hot and fry the chicken thighs and half the garlic until browned, then reduce the heat and cook for between 20–30 minutes until cooked through. Remove from the pan and set aside. Fry the onion and remaining garlic in the pan until soft, adding more oil if needed, then add the paprika and chilli, and stir. Add the tomatoes and wine and let it bubble for 30 seconds. Next add the chicken back to the pan, along with the rice, the stock and the saffron. Season very well (honestly, if you don't put enough salt in, it will be yuck!), let it bubble for 10 minutes, then add the shellfish and squid. Continue cooking for another 5–10 minutes, adding more stock if needed.

Test the rice for doneness – you want it soft but also a little nutty. Garnish with parsley and lemons and get out your castanets. (Don't just use the lemon for decoration – squeeze it over the paella and see how it makes the flavours zing!)

FONDODODODODODODO
WITH HERB SALAD

Yes, some things are best left consigned to the past, but let us not forget the fondue. There really is no better reason to gather a group of friends round a table than a pot of bubbling cheesy goodness.

Serves 6

400g Gruyère, grated

300g strong Cheddar, grated

10g cornflour

1 large garlic clove, peeled and bashed with the palm of your hand

300ml white wine – try to buy reasonable quality, it really will be worthwhile

150g cream cheese, at room temperature

a sprinkle of cayenne pepper

crusty bread, cut into cubes, to serve

FOR THE SALAD

1 tsp grain mustard

juice of 1 lemon

8 tbsp olive oil

salt and pepper

1 bunch of parsley, leaves only

1 bunch of lovage, leaves only

1 bunch of chervil, small sprigs only

handful of celery leaves

Place both grated cheeses along with the cornflour in a bowl, and toss around with your hands until the cheese is lightly coated with the flour.

Take the bashed piece of garlic and rub it all around the inside of your fondue pot. Really give it a good push to release some of the oils. Leave your pot in a warm place.

Pour the white wine into a large saucepan and bring it to the boil. Reduce the temperature so that the wine is just boiling, and begin adding the grated cheese a little at a time, using a whisk or a wooden spoon to work it into the boiling wine. Keep going until you have mixed all the cheese into the wine. With the saucepan over a very low heat, whisk or stir the cream cheese into the fondue until you have a lovely, smooth mixture. Keep warm in the saucepan on a very low heat, stirring regularly until you're ready to serve.

Meanwhile, make the salad dressing by whisking together the grain mustard, lemon juice and olive oil, until you reach a smooth consistency. Season with a little salt and pepper.

Toss together all of your lovely leaves.

When ready to serve, pour the fondue into the warmed pot, sprinkle over the cayenne pepper and deliver to the table along with the dressing, salad, bread and a knowing wink.

BREAD ALMOND GARLIC DIP

This is actually served as a soup in Spain, but I love to serve it as a dip with lots of colourful veg and a glass or two of vino!

Serves 4

200g old white bread

100g almonds (with skin on)

1 garlic clove, crushed

salt and pepper

180ml cold water

80ml good-quality olive oil

2 tsp white wine, or sherry vinegar

almonds, grapes or olives to decorate

Soak the white bread in a little water for a couple of minutes and then squeeze it out well. Cover the almonds in boiling water then, after a few minutes, pop them out of their skins. Put the nuts in a blender and blitz them as fine as you can then add the crushed garlic. Add the squeezed-out bread and seasoning and blitz again till you get a purée consistency. Blitz again as you gradually add the water followed by the oil and vinegar. Taste and see if it needs a bit more salt and then blitz till really smooth.

Chill well in the fridge and serve topped with almonds, olives or grapes with lots of veg for dipping on the side.

TEAR AND SHARE CINNAMON BUNS

These are so moreish that if your kids, husband, parents, nephews, nieces, guinea pigs and dogs are anything like mine, they will pester you daily to cook them over and over again.

Makes 8

FOR THE DOUGH

225ml milk

50g unsalted butter, cubed, plus extra for greasing

2 tbsp caster sugar

1 sachet (7g) dried active yeast

2 free-range eggs

500g strong white flour, plus extra for dusting

3g salt

FOR THE FILLING

40g unsalted butter, softened

4 tsp ground cinnamon

6 tbsp caster sugar

FOR THE ICING

80g mascarpone

60g icing sugar

2 tsp vanilla extract

3–4 tbsp warm water

Pour the milk into a jug and add the butter and caster sugar. Warm the mixture up so that the butter melts into the milk. I find the easiest way to do this is to sling the jug in the microwave for about 30 seconds, but you can use a saucepan over a low heat. When you've melted the butter into the milk, add the yeast and whisk all the ingredients together until everything is well mixed. Crack in the 2 eggs, and whisk again.

Sift the flour into a bowl with the salt, and pour in the yeast mixture. Bring the mix together, first with a spoon and then with your hands. When the dough starts to come together, tip it out onto a floured surface and knead for about 5 minutes. (The dough is quite elastic and wet, so it's a good idea to flour the surface fairly well.) Once you've kneaded the dough, put it in a bowl and cover with a tea towel or clingfilm before putting it in a warm place for 2 hours.

Make the filling by beating together the ingredients until you achieve a smooth paste.

After 2 hours, tip the dough onto a floured surface and knead for a minute to knock the air out. Use a rolling pin to roll the dough into a rectangle, roughly 40cm x 35cm, with the longer side facing you. Spread the cinnamon paste over the dough, as evenly as possible and all the way to the edges.

Pick up the edge closest to you and begin to roll the dough to make a long sausage shape. Next, cut the roll into eight. I find it easiest to cut the roll in half, then cut those two halves into four. You can now turn each portion onto its cut side to show the swirl in the middle.

Lightly grease a round 20cm-deep baking dish with butter. My dish is 28cm x 15cm, and the size is quite important as you now need to place the uncooked buns, cut side up, into the dish about 5cm from each other. Place the filled dish back in a warm place and leave to prove again for a further 35 minutes.

Preheat your oven to 200°C/gas 6.

Place the baking dish in the oven and bake the buns for 20 minutes, then reduce the heat to 180°C/gas 4 and bake for a further 20 minutes.

While the buns are baking, make your icing by beating together all the icing ingredients.

When the buns are cooked, remove them from the oven and immediately spoon over half the icing. It will melt into the buns and sit in the base of the dish – this is perfect. Leave the buns to cool to room temperature.

When ready to serve, spoon the remaining icing over the buns. Yum.

JELLY AND ICE CREAM...
WIBBLE WOBBLE WIBBLE WOBBLE

This is a great dessert to get the kids (and the grown-ups – grown-ups deserve jelly too!) involved with. Once you have turned the jelly out, let the kids decorate it – it will soon become a firm family favourite. I use cherry cordial, but this method can be adapted to accommodate almost any flavour. I also use a savarin mould to create the large doughnut shape; these are widely available online, but even a Pyrex bowl will give you a lovely shaped jelly.

Serves 6

500ml morello cherry cordial

500ml water

12 sheets of gelatine

TO DECORATE

1 tub chocolate ice cream

1 tub vanilla ice cream

raspberries

blueberries

blackberries

dark chocolate

Pour the cordial into a saucepan, and add the water. Stir to mix, and heat the liquid over a light to medium heat; do not let it boil. In the meantime, soak the gelatine leaves in a bowl of cold water. They need to sit in this water for about 5 minutes.

When the gelatine has turned soft and the diluted cordial is warm, fish the gelatine from the water and give it a good squeeze to drain off excess water. Remove the cordial from the heat, and gradually add the gelatine, stirring constantly to dissolve into the warm liquid. Once all the gelatine has dissolved, pour the cordial into a jug and let it cool to room temperature.

When the liquid has cooled, pour into your mould and carefully place in the fridge to chill for a minimum of 6 hours, but preferably overnight.

When ready to serve, pour boiling hot water into something big enough to accommodate your chosen mould – if nothing else, the sink is a good starting place. Dip your mould into the hot water for 3–5 seconds, just long enough to release the jelly. Remove the mould from the hot water, place a large plate over the top, and then in one swift movement flip the plate over. The jelly should flop onto the plate; if it doesn't, give it a good shake. If it still refuses to budge, sit the mould back in the warm water for a further few seconds.

If not eating straight away, place the jelly back in the fridge (this is a good plan). When ready to serve, decorate liberally with ice cream, fruit and grated dark chocolate.

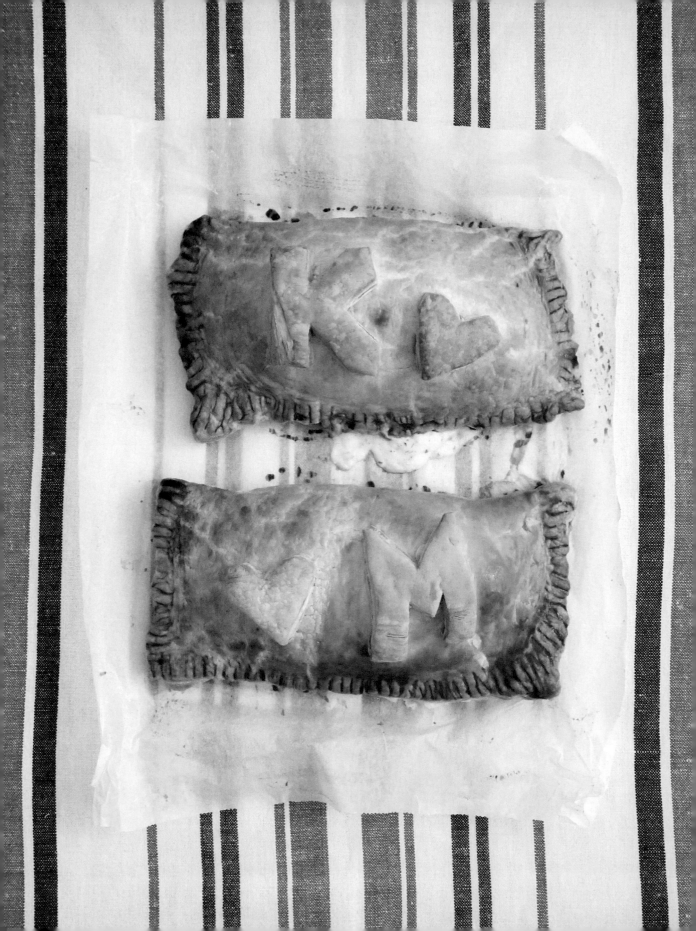

MORE PLEASE, MUM

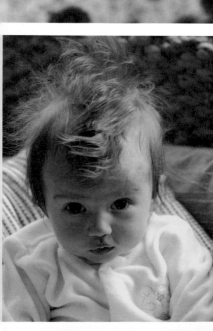

Kids: *noun, informal* a child or young person (used as a familiar form of address); a young goat

Awww, the joys, horrors, highs and lows of feeding my 'little darlings' over the last eleven years has been challenging, to say the least! I'd always imagined in my young, free and single (rose-tinted glasses) days that once I was married and 'had my own children' feeding them would be a like a scene from a fairy story.

I would let my imagination run wild as I pictured myself floating around with long multi-coloured braided hair and a billowing kaftan, straight out of some Laura Ashley hippy-style costume drama. You know the kind of things: the ultimate mother-earth figure, hip, cool and a rock 'n' role model that all your children thought of as a best friend first, a mum second! I'd whiff of home-baked bread and stewed apples; I'd be able to henna tattoo their arms at the same time as making my own pasta; play guitar and tambourine while simultaneously making chutney, jam and pickles! I envisaged my bohemian kitchen, with brightly painted shelves, bushels of dried herbs, jars of exotic-smelling spices gathered from my wild and whacked-out travelling days touring the Middle East in homage to my Bedouin roots.

My imagined future as a parent was going to be all about gazing upon my jolly rosy-cheeked babies playing happily by the warmth of my wood-fired Aga. I'd scoop my hungry little darlings up into my arms and gently lower them into their high chairs, hand-made and beautifully carved by their Adonis-like father. I'd then lovingly spoon my homemade lentil soup with a flourish of bone-building tofu and wilted spinach into their perfectly smiling rosebud lips. Their eyes would light up with the knowledge that I had nourished them in the very best way possible and they would, of course, love every mouthful . . . CUT . . . Yeah, right! The only part of the above fantasy that in any way comes close to reality is (of course) the being married to an Adonis (wink wink, Mark!). The rest – well – it didn't even make it to pipe-dream status!

Feeding my little darlings was (and still is) so far removed from this imagined idyll that I'm almost embarrassed to write another word! It is a reality of struggles, fights, rows, negotiations, strops, slamming doors, tears, squeals, pleas, prayers, bribes, threats, lies, blackmails, exaggerations, explanations, broken crockery, fork injuries, thrown vegetables, burnt potatoes, hair-pullings, punched husbands . . . Need I go on?

These are my top recipes to keep them quiet and have them begging for more.

NB All the serving instructions are with two adults, two children in mind.

BISH AND KNOCKERS

Confused by the title? I'm not surprised! This was named by Kiki-Bee, as she couldn't say fish and gnocchi. This is a healthy way to make fish and chips that's also far easier than frying . . . oh, and it's delicious!

Mark and I love to have a tomato salad with this – of course, the girls would rather leave home than eat a tomato salad.

Serves 4

3 slices of stale white bread

2 tbsp plain flour

salt and pepper

1–2 free-range eggs, whisked

2 tbsp lemon juice

4 sustainable white fish fillets (such as haddock, hoki, pollock)

a couple of glugs of vegetable oil

400g gnocchi

Preheat the oven to 200°C/gas 6.

Put the bread in a blender and then pulse into breadcrumbs. Place on a plate.

Put the flour on another plate and season with salt and pepper. Pour the eggs into a shallow bowl.

Sprinkle the lemon juice over the fish, then roll in the flour, dip in the egg and then into the breadcrumbs. Put on a greased baking tray and bake in the oven for 20 minutes or until the breadcrumbs are golden and the fish is cooked through.

10 minutes after you have put the fish in the oven, heat the oil in a frying pan, add the gnocchi and fry on both sides until golden. Serve with the fish and whatever veg you can get your 'little darlings' to eat!

SWEETIE PORK

OK, I'm a bad mother! But calling this 'sweetie' pork gets my youngest to eat it. The sweetie bit comes from the roast apples, and Kiki lurves apples . . . she's OK about pork . . . but lurves apples!

Serves 4

8–10 new potatoes, halved

2 red onions, quartered

2 eating apples, cored and quartered (peeling them makes them easier to eat but they look better unpeeled – your choice)

salt and pepper

a good drizzle of olive oil

4 small pork escalopes

Preheat the oven to 200°C/gas 6.

Parboil the potatoes in salted water until just tender. Then drain them and put in a roasting tin with the onions and apples. Sprinkle with salt and pepper and drizzle with the olive oil. Roast for 25–30 minutes or until the fruit and vegetables are golden and tender.

Dry the pork with kitchen paper then put into a sandwich bag or wrap in clingfilm so you can bash them flat with a rolling pin! Heat up a griddle pan (a heavy-based frying pan is fine too), rub a little oil onto the pork and season well. Then throw onto the pan and cook for a couple of minutes on each side (or until cooked through). Be careful not to overcook or they will dry out. Serve with the roasted veg and apples.

GARLIC BREAD CHICKEN PIES

Now there is no garlic bread involved here but my girls used to call anything that tasted of garlic 'garlic bread' when they were small, and it's stuck with this super-easy, super-yummy chicken with a twist.

Serves 4

4 chicken breasts

½ clove garlic, very finely chopped (optional)

250g garlic- and herb-flavoured cream cheese

salt and pepper

1.3kg puff pastry

1 free-range egg, whisked with a little milk

Preheat the oven to 190°C/gas 5.

Take the skin off the chicken. Using a sharp knife, make a pocket in the chicken breasts.

Mix the garlic into the cream cheese (but only if you want extra garlic, of course!). Then stuff the pockets in the chicken breasts equally with the herby cheese. Season the chicken.

Using a rolling pin on a lightly floured surface, roll out the pastry and cut into four squares big enough to completely cover the chicken. Then put one of the breasts at the bottom of the pastry and, starting at one corner, roll the pastry over until it overlaps and encases each stuffed chicken breast. Pinch down the sides and score the edges with a fork. Repeat with the remaining chicken.

Brush the chicken parcels with the egg mix. Pop onto a baking tray and bake in the oven for 35–40 minutes. The pastry should look beautifully golden.

I usually serve this with steamed carrots tossed in a little butter, chopped parsley and shallot. Failing that, peas are good – oh, and so is mash!

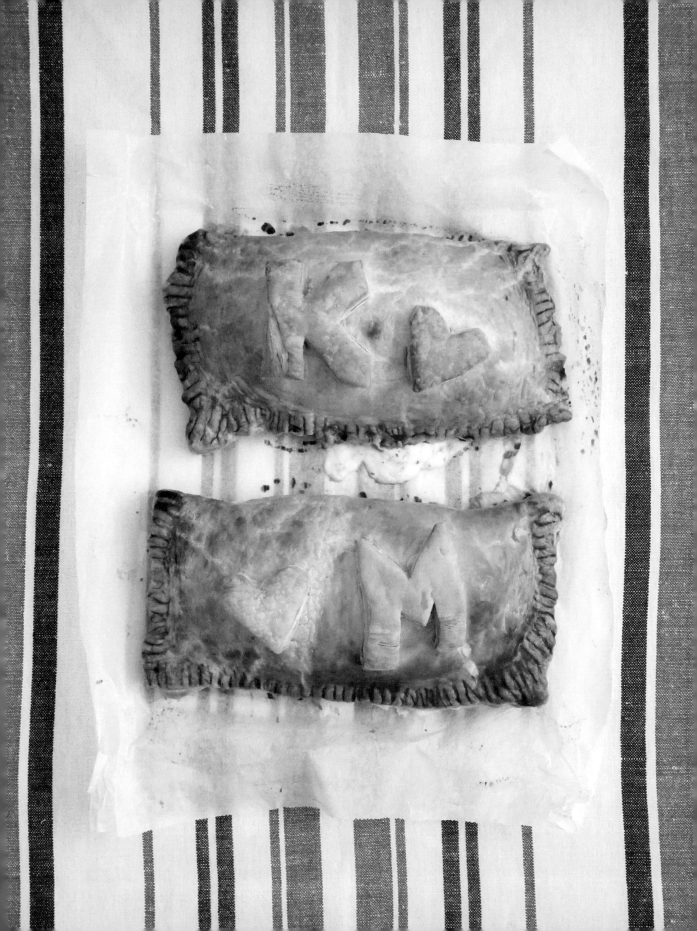

KIDDIE ROAST VEG WITH GARLIC MAYO

OK, so I know I've cheated here by using all 'sweet' veg to get it down my 'little darlings" throats, but hey, a girl's gotta do what a girl's gotta do!

Serves 4

6 small carrots

4 small parsnips

2 sweet potatoes, cut into 6 wedges

½ swede, cut into 2.5cm wedges

2 red peppers, cut into quarters lengthways

6 garlic cloves

4 tbsp olive oil

FOR THE GARLIC MAYO

1 garlic clove, very finely chopped

8 tbsp mayonnaise

Preheat the oven to 220°C/gas 7.

Toss the vegetables and garlic cloves in the olive oil, lay out on a large baking tray (or two, as you don't want the veg to sweat rather than roast) and put in the oven for 35–40 minutes.

Meanwhile, make the garlic mayo. Stir the garlic into the mayo – easy, huh! Serve the roasted veg with the mayo to dip.

TWO-DAYS-IN-A-ROW ROAST

My girls' number-one, top of the game, most favourite meal ever is a chicken roast dinner with all the trimmings! If they could, they would have it every day, which would of course be impossible! But I have found a way for them to at least have it two days running. I basically heat up the leftovers from any chicken roast we have in a good-quality gravy and then pile it all into their own homemade Yorkshire puds, and they love it! OK then, I will now take a bow!

NB Please, please, please make sure the fat is smoking hot, if you want well-risen puds. You have been warned!

Serves 4–6

FOR THE PUDS
250g plain flour, sifted
pinch of salt
4 free-range eggs, beaten
150ml full-fat milk, mixed in a jug with 150ml water
vegetable oil or dripping

FOR THE FILLING
400ml good-quality gravy
leftover chicken
8 leftover mini pork sausages
leftover stuffing balls
100g petits pois

Preheat the oven to 230°C/gas 8.

Put the flour and salt into a mixing bowl. Make a well in the middle and add the beaten eggs. Gradually stir the milk and water mix into the bowl and whisk until all lumps have vanished. The batter should be thick enough to coat the back of a spoon. Don't be afraid to add a little more milk if it looks too thick. I try to leave it to rest for 15 minutes, but often forget and have to use it straight away! It's a good idea to transfer it to a jug so you can pour it easily into the hot fat later on.

Pour about ½ teaspoon vegetable oil into each mould of a six-hole muffin tin. Heat in the hot oven until the oil is smoking hot. Once it's hot enough, act quickly (if possible, it's a good idea to put the tin on the hob to keep the oil really hot), pouring in the batter – if the fat doesn't sizzle with the first drop, put the oil back into the oven – until each mould is three-quarters full then get them back into the oven as fast as possible.

Cook for 20–25 minutes until risen, puffy and golden. Don't open the oven too early, or you WILL pass out!

Pour the gravy into a saucepan along with the chicken, sausages and stuffing and gently simmer until they are piping hot in the middle. Cook the peas according to packet instructions. Pile everything into the Yorkshire puds and you're good to go!

KIND OF BOLOGNAISE PIE

Now God forbid if this dish ever replaced spaghetti bolognaise on a permanent basis, but every so often it makes a really nice change. How brave am I!

Serves 4

500g lean beef mince

2 tbsp olive oil

1 large onion, finely chopped

2 celery sticks, finely chopped

2 garlic cloves, crushed

3 tbsp tomato purée

1 large glass of wine

400g tin plum tomatoes

salt and pepper

1 bay leaf

375g ready-rolled puff pastry

milk for brushing

Heat a large frying pan and fry the meat in batches until it's nicely browned. Set aside. Add the oil to the pan and heat through. Throw in the onion and celery and cook until soft but not browned, then add the garlic and cook until softened and aroma released. Now add the tomato purée and fry for 1–2 minutes (you want it to change colour for it to be ready), stirring the whole time.

Put the meat back in the pan, pour in the wine and bubble until the wine is reduced. Add the tin of tomatoes to the pan, half-fill the tin with water and add that too. Now season well, add the bay leaf and let it pop and bubble away on a very low heat for 45–60 minutes, adding more water if it looks dry.

Half an hour before you want to eat, preheat the oven to 200°C/gas 6. Cut the pastry into four big hearts, brush with milk, then put on a baking tray. Pop into the oven and cook for 15–20 minutes or until puffed and golden. Serve the bolognaise sauce topped with the pastry. Yum!

NO JUNK ALPHABETTI SPAGHETTI

The kids love this pasta, not only because they can play spelling games but also because it's delish! Mark and I love it too, but we add lots of torn basil and Parmesan to ours!

Serves 4

350g alphabet pasta

grated cheese (whatever they will eat)

FOR THE VEGGIE TOMATO SAUCE

(This will make more sauce than you need, so you can either keep it in the fridge or freeze for another day.)

3 carrots, peeled

3 courgettes (peel if the 'little darlings' don't eat green bits)

½ butternut squash, peeled and deseeded

3 tbsp olive oil

3 garlic cloves, finely chopped

2 x 400g tins tomatoes

pinch of sugar

sea salt and pepper

Start with the sauce. Using a food processor, grate the carrots, courgettes and butternut squash. Heat the oil in a large pan over a medium heat, add the garlic and fry until just softened. Then add the grated vegetables and cook and stir until softened. Pour in the tomatoes then fill the tins with water and add that. Add the sugar and season well. Bring up to the bubble then reduce the heat and simmer for 45 minutes.

Cook the pasta according to packet instructions. When cooked, drain and stir in some of the tomato veggie sauce. Top with grated cheese.

HONEY STICKY CHICKEN NOODLES

Come on, what kids don't love sweet sticky things? But with this dish there is also a good whack of protein and carbs, and veg too!

Now you can swap the chicken for duck, which I love, but my 'little darlings' don't!

Serves 4

3 tbsp clear honey

2 tbsp water

3 tbsp dark soy sauce

1 tbsp cornflour

4 skinless chicken breasts

2 carrots

6–8 spring onions (leave out if the kids hate 'green bits')

1 tbsp vegetable oil

handful of petits pois

1 garlic clove, grated (optional)

noodles and 1–2 tbsp sesame oil, to serve

Mix together the honey, soy sauce, water and cornflour in a large bowl. Slice the chicken into strips and then toss in the honey marinade. Cut the carrots (having got your 'little darling' to peel them first) and spring onions into thin strips.

Heat the vegetable oil in a wok or large frying pan. Take the chicken out of the marinade with a slotted spoon and stir-fry for 2 minutes until slightly browned all over, then remove it (again with the slotted spoon) and put in a warmed bowl. Add the carrot, petits pois and garlic (if using) and stir-fry for 1 minute. Add the spring onion, then return the chicken to the pan. Pour the marinade in and stir-fry for a couple of minutes. Serve with noodles tossed in sesame oil.

PRETTY PESTO PASTA

Right, I am going to be honest here: although the girls love this super-easy dish they both hate the pine nuts bit so I simply sprinkle them on mine and Mark's at the end – oh, and 'no olives' on Maddie's! Right! Is everyone happy now?

PS This is so easy!

Serves 4

600g pretty-looking pasta

2 avocados

juice of ½ lemon (or more, taste and see)

zest of 1 lemon

6 heaped tbsp pesto

2 x 200g tins tuna in oil, drained

handful of green olives

4 tbsp toasted pine nuts

black pepper (optional)

Cook the pasta as directed and while it's happily cooking away, peel and cube the avocados and put in a salad bowl with the lemon juice and zest. Add the pesto, drained tuna and the olives. Now add the pasta and give a good stir before sprinkling with the toasted pine nuts and some freshly ground black pepper if you fancy a little bite! I like to have a green salad alongside mine – but no one else does . . . Grrrr.

SPOIL-YOURSELF SUNDAY BREAKFASTS

Break-fast: *noun* a meal eaten in the morning, the first of the day

Breakfast! Such a wonderfully appropriate word for the thing it describes: that moment in the morning when we all quite literally 'break' our nocturnal 'fasts'. Hoorah! There's something wild and primal about morning hunger. Your body is depleted, you feel at your most vulnerable as you awaken and stumble out into the world. It's a time of half-light, tip-toeing, hushed questions, tousled hair, bleary eyes and the occasional throbbing brain.

In our household (as I'm sure is the case in many of yours), mornings can be tricky. Whilst two of us (me and Kiki-Bee) are very firmly what you'd call morning animals, the other two (Maddie and Mark) are very much . . . NOT! Kiki and I wake up chattering and chirruping as if we were midway through a conversation at a party but Mark and Maddie look and sound as though they've had to summon their very souls up from beneath the kitchen table in order to open their eyes, brush back their hair and even acknowledge that Kiki and I exist!

Maddie and Mark are what we call slow-burners in the morning. In fact my two step-daughters, Isobel and Fleur, are exactly the same, so it is definitely a morning trait that has emerged from Mark's genetic make-up – NOT MINE! As you can well imagine, having some very fragile souls in our household every morning, I have to be on my toes when it comes to 'suggesting' what they eat for breakfast. The one thing you don't want to do with any of them is 'break' their 'fasts' in the wrong way. Now some mornings they sleepwalk around the kitchen, grunting to any questions, whilst pouring some awful cereal (I didn't buy it!) into a bowl and splashing some milk over the top before sitting down, munching and staring blank-eyed into the distance. This is what I refer to as their zombie breakfast.

Other mornings, however, they come down slightly out of sorts but with a grudging acknowledgement that if they don't alienate me too much, I may well work my magic in the kitchen and deliver them something to eat that has the potential to transform not only their morning but their entire day!

In order to avoid divorce or putting Maddie up for adoption, I need to win them over, break down their harsh exteriors and release the lovely people that Kiki-Bee and I know them to be. It might not be easy but the upside for you reading this chapter is that the entire process has resulted in some very inventive culinary treats that I am sure will work wonders on any moody person you happen to have sitting at your breakfast table!

With regards to me and Kiki-Bee (us ever-happy morning-munchers), well, what can I say? Breakfast for us eternal optimists is an oasis of opportunity – a chance to stand with the fridge door held wide, wondering what culinary treats we can pull together, and what flavour combos will make us even happier and chattier than we were when we first got up!

So here you go, my lovelies, my Sunday break-fasts with love . . .

CHEESY EGG 'N' BACON MUFFINS

Forgive my shameless showing off here, but I think I've been really clever with this recipe!

Makes 6

6 free-range hard-boiled eggs

150g pancetta cubes

300g plain flour, plus a little extra to dust

1 tbsp baking powder

1 large free-range egg

100g strong cheddar cheese, grated

200ml milk

50ml olive oil

good pinch of salt

Preheat the oven to 190C/gas 5. Line 6 large muffin tins with paper cases.

Dust the hard-boiled eggs in a little flour (this helps the mixture to stick to them). Heat a frying pan and cook the pancetta until it just starts to brown (we don't want the pieces to brown too much as they will cook again in the oven). Take them off the heat and set them to one side.

Sieve the flour and baking powder into a large bowl. In a separate bowl, whisk together the egg, cheese, milk, olive oil and salt.

Fold the egg mixture into the flour bowl with most of the pancetta. Fold for no more than 10 seconds as too much folding will give you tough, misshapen muffins. Then place a small spoonful of the mixture into the bottom of each of the cases. Sit the hard-boiled eggs on top, then spoon the remaining mixture over the top.

Sprinkle with the reserved pancetta and bake in the centre of the oven for 20–25 minutes, or until risen and golden brown.

EGG 'N' STREAKING SOLDIERS

Egg, bacon and bread. Need I say more?

Serves 4

½ an uncut white loaf

4 thin rashers smoked streaky bacon, halved widthways

vegetable oil for frying

4 large free-range eggs

salt and pepper

You will need four 2–2.5cm-thick slices of bread with the crusts removed. Then cut each slice of bread into three wide fingers and twist a piece of bacon around the length of each one.

Heat a large non-stick frying pan over a high heat and add a little vegetable oil. Once the oil is hot add the bacon bread fingers, seam-side down, and fry on each side until nice and golden.

Meanwhile, put the eggs into a pan and cover with cold water. Bring to the boil over a high heat and immediately start timing. Boil for 3 minutes for a very soft runny yolk to dip your gorgeous soldiers in to your heart's content.

THE ULTIMATE BLT – BUT EVEN BETTER BECAUSE OF THE AVOCADO!

Now this baby is my very own favourite spoil-yourself breakfast and I'm beyond fussy about it. The streaky bacon must be of an American standard, super-thin and deeply smoked. The tomatoes and avocado must be perfectly ripe, and the bread, perfectly toasted . . . Unsurprisingly no one, but no one, has the courage to make said sarnie for me – I wonder why!

Serves 4

16 rashers smoked streaky bacon, rind removed

8 slices of your favourite unhealthy bread

4 tbsp good-quality mayonnaise

8 iceberg lettuce leaves

2 large tomatoes, sliced

1 large avocado, sliced

Grill the bacon rashers until they are perfectly crispy, and lightly toast the bread. Now spread half the mayo on 4 slices of the toast and layer a lettuce leaf and tomato and avocado on top of each slice before topping it all with the bacon, another lettuce leaf, a dollop of mayo and a second slice of toast.

EGGS BENEDICT

This is my husband's all-time favourite spoil-yourself brekkie. It is a bit faffy (I sometimes have to resist the urge to say, 'Are you sure you don't just want toast, babe?') but he is so lovely I don't mind spoiling him – as long as it's not more than once a year!

Serves 2

FOR THE HOLLANDAISE SAUCE

150ml dry white wine

225ml white wine vinegar

15 whole black peppercorns

1 small onion, finely chopped

250g unsalted butter

3 free-range egg yolks

FOR THE EGGS

3 tbsp white wine vinegar

2 very fresh free-range eggs

2 English muffins, sliced in half, toasted

2 slices ham

100g baby spinach leaves, wilted

To whip up your hollandaise: Put the wine, vinegar, peppercorns and onion into a heavy-based pan set on a high heat. Bring it all up to the boil and reduce the liquid by half. This will take about 15 minutes.

While the wine and vinegar mixture is reducing, put the butter in a small heavy-based pan and melt over a low heat. When the butter has melted, using a spoon, skim the white foamy bits from the surface and discard. Remove the butter from the heat and cool it down to lukewarm.

Place a glass bowl over a pan of simmering water. Don't let the water touch the bottom of the bowl, though. Now put the egg yolks in the bowl and whisk. Add about 1 tablespoon of the vinegar and onion reduction. Whisk the egg yolk mixture constantly for about 5 minutes, until it turns foamy and thickens. The mixture is ready when it falls from the whisk in strands that rest for a second or two on the surface.

Take the egg mixture off the heat. Pour a small amount of the lukewarm melted butter into the egg mixture and whisk vigorously until the butter is completely incorporated. Gradually add the rest of the butter to the egg mixture, whisking it all in until a smooth, thick sauce is formed.

To make a damn fine poached egg: Fill a deep pan with water. Bring to the boil and add the white wine vinegar. Make a 'whirlpool' in the pan by swirling a slotted spoon around the outside edge of the water. Carefully crack the eggs into the pan in the centre of the whirlpool, take off the heat and leave for 3–4 minutes until the whites are done. I always give them a prod with a wooden spoon and if they are firm then they are ready.

To serve, put half a lightly toasted muffin on each plate. Top with a slice of ham (Mark only likes the ham if it's cold but feel free to fry it if you prefer), the spinach (well drained and left on a piece of kitchen paper to remove any last drops of water) and a poached egg. Spoon hollandaise over the egg and around the muffin. Place the other muffin half on the top and serve immediately.

MUESLI MILK 'N' COOKIES

Awww, my baby girl Kiki-Bee (come on, Nadia, she's six now!) loves to make these biscuits with me, and that ain't all about quality time with Mama. Oh no, she's far more her mother's daughter than that. My 'little angel' truly believes that when she makes something she's entitled to eat twice as much of it as anyone else! By the way, if you could see me as I write this, you would see that I'm positively beaming with pride. That's my girl!

Makes 20-25

170g soft butter

170g self-raising flour

100g caster sugar

½ tsp ground ginger or cinnamon

1 large free-range egg, whisked

170g muesli

60g flaked almonds

organic full-fat milk, hot or cold, to serve

Warm up that oven of yours to 180°C/gas 4. Now lightly grease a baking tray so it's ready to meet the biscuits!

Put the butter, flour, sugar, ginger or cinnamon, and egg into a large bowl and beat together until it's nice and smooth. Sprinkle in your muesli and stir it all up.

Using a teaspoon, plop spoonfuls of the mixture onto the baking tray but, be warned, they will spread so leave them room to do that in peace! Sprinkle the bickies with the flaked almonds and bake for about 10–15 minutes or until they are golden brown.

Leave on the tray for a few minutes before trying to put them on a cooling rack otherwise they might fall apart a little. Once cool, enjoy with a mug of milk.

GRANNY'S GRANOLA

This is my mum Betty's recipe, so consequently my girls love to sometimes pop next door on a Sunday to Granny's for breakfast! It will make about 1.5kg but the good news is that it can be stored at room temperature in an airtight container for up to 1 month. Be warned though, you may (if you're anything like me) find yourself raiding it late at night!

Makes 1.5kg

125g unsalted butter

170ml honey

1½ tsp vanilla extract

500g rolled oats

1 cup sunflower seeds (I use a good-sized teacup instead of American cups for the measures in this recipe, which is much easier)

½ cup sesame seeds

1 cup flaked almonds

½ cup chopped pecan nuts

½ cup desiccated coconut

¾ cup pumpkin seeds

1 cup chopped dried fruit – I like dates, sultanas, raisins and cranberries but it's all about what you like, not me!

Put the butter, honey and vanilla in a small saucepan. Cook gently over a low heat, giving it a stir until the honey and butter are melted.

Put the remaining ingredients, except the fruit, in a large mixing bowl and mix thoroughly. Slowly pour in the butter mixture, stirring well to make sure that everything is evenly coated.

Spread your granola mix over two baking trays and bake in the oven for 25 minutes, or until the grains are very lightly golden. I usually give it all a bit of a stir halfway through to stop it from sticking. Once it's looking lovely, take it out of the oven and let it cool, then add your dried fruit and give it a final good stir.

TREACLE AND TAHINI WITH HOT PITTA BREAD

This recipe is a real taste of my childhood – my sisters and I used to love this breakfast treat when we were kids. It was what my dad used to have (once a year – they were very poor) when he was growing up. And now my girls love it too.

The added bonus here is that blackstrap molasses is very rich in iron, and tahini is pure calcium, so while the kids happily eat it because it's delicious they have no idea (that would spoil some of the fun) that it's really good for them too. Strike one to Mum!

Serves 4

4 small pitta breads

4 tbsp blackstrap molasses (this can be found in any good health food shop)

2 tbsp tahini

Heat the pitta bread under the grill or in the toaster until it's lovely and warm. Then drizzle the molasses and tahini separately on four small plates and mop up with the pitta bread. Yum. xx

DOMESTIC GODDESS BREAD

Go on, unleash the domestic goddess (sorry, Nigella, you can't be the only one!) that lurks within you and get baking. Baking bread always makes me happy because I love kneading (I really, really love it). This loaf is divine, packed full of dried fruit and seeds and infused with the fragrance of Earl Grey – another Sawalha favourite.

Makes 1 loaf

60g dried cranberries

60g dried cherries

60g raisins

400ml Earl Grey tea, made with 2 teabags and steeped for 3 minutes

2 tsp soft dark brown sugar

1 sachet (7g) dried active yeast

500g strong wholemeal bread flour, plus a little extra for dusting

30g porridge oats

30g pumpkin seeds

6g salt

50g soft butter

Tip the cranberries, cherries and raisins into a bowl and pour over about 100ml of the still warm Earl Grey (this doesn't have to be exact as all the liquid will end up in the bread). Leave the fruit to soak for at least 10 minutes.

In the meantime add the sugar and yeast to the remaining lukewarm tea and stir well to dissolve the dry ingredients. Leave this to stand.

Put the flour, oats, pumpkin seeds, salt and butter into a bowl. Mix lightly with a fork.

Pour the yeast and sugar-enhanced tea into the bowl with the dry ingredients and, using your fork, roughly mix them together. Tip in the steeped fruits with the liquid, and again roughly mix with a fork.

Next, generously dust a clean surface with some of the extra flour and tip the dough onto it. Knead the dough for about 5 minutes, or until you are satisfied all of the ingredients are well combined.

Roll your already lovely dough up into a ball and put into a clean bowl. Lightly cover the bowl with a clean tea towel and put in a warm place for about 1½ hours, by which time the dough should have doubled in size.

Once your dough has doubled, tip it out onto a clean surface and knead for another 2 minutes to knock the air out. Shape into a large torpedo shape, before dropping into a loaf tin. Let the dough rise in a warm place again for about 35 minutes, by which time it should begin to rise out of the tin.

Preheat your oven to 190°C/gas 5.

When your loaf has risen, slash across the top with a very sharp knife in three places and place in the oven. Bake for 40 minutes then reduce the heat to 170°C/gas 3 and bake for a further 10 minutes. The whole house will smell like bakery heaven.

Remove your loaf from the oven. Tip it out onto a clean surface and give the base a tap. The loaf is ready when it sounds hollow. If you are unsure, replace it in the oven for a further 10 minutes.

The berries that are on the top of the loaf will be burnt to a crisp and should be discarded, as they will be bitter. Enjoy your bread warm with lashings of butter.

Spoil-Yourself Sunday Breakfasts | **165**

NUTELLA-STUFFED PANCAKES

My husband has such an intense addiction to Nutella that if he gets wind that there is a jar of it in the house he either hurls it (WHILST RUNNING AND SCREAMING) into next-door's garden or he simply tears into it and eats the lot with his bare hands. Well, anyway, both our daughters, through nature or nurture (I'm not sure which), have inherited the same out of control addiction! So on birthdays ONLY this is what my little brood of addicts get from their Mama/Missus.

Serves 4, makes 8 pancakes

225g plain flour

1 tbs baking powder

2 tsp caster sugar

300ml milk

2 large free-range eggs

spray vegetable oil for frying

Nutella!

Simply put all the ingredients, except the Nutella, into a blender and blitz until you have a smooth batter.

Heat a non-stick frying pan and spray with a thin film of oil. Put a spoonful of the pancake mixture into the pan and then a little blob of Nutella in the middle. Spoon a little more batter over the Nutella to seal it. Once you see bubbles forming, and the batter drying around the edges, flip it and cook on the other side.

Put onto a warm plate while you finish cooking all the mixture. And there you have it – my family's drug of choice on their plates for all to see!

PS Sliced bananas, as you can imagine, go rather well.

SPICED POACHED FRUIT

As my parents only live next door we sometimes (à la the Waltons) have breakfast together on a Sunday and if the 'party' is at mine I whip up this gorgeous dish of poached fruits for my mum as she loves it. But she has become extremely decadent in recent years and demands double cream to be drizzled over the fruit rather than Greek yogurt. Ahhh the bonuses of old age!

Serves 4

2 litres cold water

1 cinnamon stick

4 whole star anise

400g golden caster sugar (just use plain caster if you haven't got any golden)

4 ripe peaches

4 ripe plums

2 pears, peeled and quartered

handful of grapes, sliced

AND THE REST

Greek yogurt

flaked toasted almonds (if you fancy)

Pour 2 litres cold water into a large saucepan and then throw in the cinnamon stick, star anise and sugar, stir well, and bring it up to the boil. Lower the heat and simmer, stirring now and again, until the sugar has dissolved into a syrup.

Add those peachy peaches to the syrup, cover the pan with a lid, reduce the heat to a simmer and leave it bubbling for 5 minutes. Then add the plums and pears and simmer for another 10 minutes, or until the fruit is perfectly soft when poked with a knife. Add the grapes in the last couple of minutes.

Using a slotted spoon, take out the fruit and set aside. Boil the syrup until it is reduced to a syrupy syrup (about a cupful). Then leave it to cool or don't, depending on what you prefer.

Drizzle a little syrup over the fruit, and spoon some creamy Greek yogurt alongside. Sprinkle with toasted almonds for a final bit of spoiling.

BAKING

Bake: *verb* to cook or dry heat in an oven or on heated metal or stones

I was never the baker in the family. In fact, up until ten years ago, I positively railed against the fuss and nonsense of baking a cake. When *The Great British Bake Off* first hit our TV screens I even dismissed it as a twee indulgence until, finally, I watched an episode. And well – naturally – just like everyone else I was hooked!

Why was I so resistant to this art form? Well part of it was the fact that it is so associated with gingham and all things village fete-like. It's just all a bit pink and girly and, to be quite frank, sissy! But I have come to realize that my resistance was (and sometimes still is) due to good old-fashioned fear!

My mum was a fantastic baker, just as good at making cakes as pies, and she regularly made bread, croissants and all manner of perfect pastries. So – whilst I loved eating her food – I was (from the off) programmed to resist the art of baking as a simple act of childhood/adolescent rebellion. It was Mum's thing! Grrrr!

So – surprise, surprise – baking first came properly into my life when I too finally became a mum. But we were (for many years) unlikely bedfellows. If it hadn't been for the ever-growing audience of expectant little faces, all with little growling bellies to satisfy, then the universe of baking would never have opened up and stretched out before me like a marzipan-and-butter-cream-covered oasis of sugary opportunities.

When I became a mum, I went from having no children to almost immediately having three daughters! My husband, whom I had met only a year before we had Maddie, already had two other daughters (who I consider to be as much my girls as they are Mark's). So from a standing start I went from zero to three kids. And with three kids goes an enormous appetite for . . . cakes!

The wonder of cake is a mysterious and slightly frightening thing. Of all the recipes one writes, with a cake recipe you need to get things absolutely right. If you make the slightest error in ingredients or amounts, the science of baking will bite you on the backside. And, as many of you will know, Hell hath no fury like a cake recipe that goes wrong. But the magic of cakes – what I love about them – is that, despite the precision required, they always look as though they've just appeared and come into being of their own free will. Like a pop-up book, a cake quite literally pings into the world and always manages to brighten the day.

They always come out at a celebration. No other dish looks more like it was always meant to be at the party than a cake. They're the main attraction, and because they're invariably the A-List Culinary Celebrity at every party, they're frightening to make. As a consequence I take cake-making very seriously these days. Indeed, it's not unheard of for me to disappear for almost four days prior to a birthday in order to start constructing my masterpiece! So rest assured, the following recipes have all been stress tested by me – and then eaten stress free by my lovely daughters (and, of course, my husband on the quiet too!).

PASTEL LAYER CAKE

I don't think I need say very much about this cake – the photo says it all!

**300g butter, cubed, at
room temperature**

350g sugar

**6 free-range eggs, lightly
whisked**

2 tsp vanilla extract

**350g self-raising flour,
sifted**

splash of milk

**food colouring: pink,
yellow, green and blue**

FOR THE BUTTER ICING

300g unsalted butter

700g icing sugar

Preheat your oven to 180°C/gas 4 and grease and line two 18cm cake tins with baking parchment.

Place the butter and sugar into a bowl and, using an electric whisk, beat the two ingredients together until the butter has turned pale. This takes about 3–4 minutes. With the whisk still running, add the eggs a little at a time. Stop whisking, pour in the vanilla extract and tip in the flour.

Use a spatula or wooden spoon to fold the flour into the rest of the ingredients. The mixture may become very firm at this point, in which case add a few splashes of milk so that the batter reaches a 'dropping' consistency.

Next for the maths. Weigh your cake batter and whatever your amount comes to, you need to divide it by 4 – in your head or on a calculator. For example, I ended up with 1280g of cake mixture, so IF your batter was the same weight as mine, then each of your cakes will take 320g of batter.

Dollop two measures of cake batter into two separate bowls, and to each bowl add a different colour. Mix the colouring in before transferring to the greased cake tins. Place your tins into the preheated oven and bake for about 20 minutes, by which time the sponges should be fully cooked through.

Leave the cakes to cool a little in their tins. This gives you time to repeat the weighing and colouring process. Remove the cakes from their tins and leave to cool on a wire rack, while you re-grease and line your tins, and reload with the next coloured cake mixtures. Bake as before. You will end up with four different-coloured cakes, which now need to cool completely.

To make the butter icing, place the butter in a bowl and beat until soft. Gradually mix in the icing sugar with 1 tablespoon hot water and continue beating for a further 3 minutes until the icing is lovely and smooth and very pale. Layer the cake, spreading the icing equally as you go. Use a palette knife to create attractive peaks on the top and outside layer.

JAMMY COCONUTTY CAKE

Loaf cakes are the way forward if you're not that confident with baking . . . I'm not sure why, but they never go wrong. This is my nephew Finlay's favourite auntie treat, and as I adore him I make it more than I probably should!

Serves 6–8

FOR THE CAKE

175g self-raising flour, sifted

175g butter, cubed, at room temperature

175g caster sugar

3 free-range eggs, whisked

50g desiccated coconut

juice of ½ large lemon

1 tbsp vanilla extract

1 tsp baking powder

FOR THE TOPPING

4–6 tbsp strawberry or raspberry jam

3 tbsp desiccated coconut

Preheat the oven to 180°C/gas 4. Line a 900g loaf tin with baking parchment.

Put all the cake ingredients in a large bowl and, using an electric whisk, whisk until you have a smooth batter. Pour into the loaf tin. Bake for 45–50 minutes. You can test whether it is done by inserting a skewer into the middle of the cake – if it comes out clean the cake's ready. Leave to stand in the tin for 10 minutes then put on a wire rack to cool.

Once cooled, spread with jam and sprinkle the coconut on top. As you can see from the photo, things can get sticky very fast!

LEMON, LIME AND POPPY SEED CAKE

This, to my utter astonishment, is one of Kiki-Bee's top cakes. My astonishment is down to the fact that it has 'bits' in! And she never touches 'bits'.

Serves 8–10

225g unsalted butter (make sure it's nice and soft)

225g caster sugar

4 free-range eggs, lightly whisked

225g self-raising flour, sifted

zest of 1½ lemons

3 tbsp poppy seeds

DRIZZLY BIT
juice of 2 limes
80g caster sugar

Preheat the oven to 180°C/gas 4. Grease a 450g loaf tin and line with baking parchment.

Put the butter and sugar into a large bowl and whisk until it's really pale and fluffy. I use my stand-alone mixer for this but if you don't have one an electric hand whisk will make light work of it. Now add the eggs a little at a time, whisking and alternating with a tablespoon of the measured flour. Then fold in the lemon zest, poppy seeds and the rest of the flour and mix well. Spoon into the prepared tin and bake for 45–55 minutes. Test whether the cake is done by inserting a skewer into the middle if it – if it comes out clean it's ready.

Make the drizzly bit by mixing the lime juice and sugar. Then prick the top of the warm cake all over with a fork and pour the drizzle over the top. Don't take the cake out of the tin until it's completely cooled.

LAVENDER SHORTBREAD

I make these biscuits for any of the girls' teachers that we really, really like!
The super-talented ones . . . the ones that deserve a medal. You know who
you are, Mr Staplehurst, Mrs Chandler, Mr Vote!

Makes 6 biscuits

125g butter, softened

**55g caster sugar, plus
extra for sprinkling**

180g plain flour

zest of 1 lemon

**1 tbsp baking lavender,
plus extra for sprinkling**

Using a wooden spoon, beat the butter and sugar together until you have
a nice smooth mixture then stir in the flour, lemon zest, lavender and a
pinch of salt.

Gently roll out the dough (be careful not to overwork it) until it's 2.5cm
thick. Then cut into rounds using a 5cm cutter. Pop onto a baking tray and
leave in the fridge for 30 minutes.

Preheat the oven to 190°C/gas 5.

Bake for 15–20 minutes then sprinkle with more sugar and lavender and
allow to cool.

FORGET-ME-NOT SPICED HONEY AND ORANGE BLOSSOM CAKES

How beautiful are these babies. If you don't have any forget-me-nots . . . cry!

Makes 6

150g butter, plus extra for greasing

175g runny honey

80g dark brown sugar

1 tbsp orange blossom water

200g plain flour, sifted

1½ tsp baking powder

1 tsp orange zest

2 tsp ground cinnamon

grated nutmeg

2 free-range eggs

FOR THE ICING

125g butter, softened

225g icing sugar

½ tbsp orange juice

½ tsp orange zest

FOR THE DECORATION

forget-me-not flowers

Grease a six-hole muffin tray or line with paper cases.

Put the butter, honey, sugar and flower water into a small pan and heat gently until the sugar is dissolved. Pour into a jug and leave to cool for about 20 minutes.

Preheat the oven to 180°C/gas 4.

Sift the flour, baking powder, orange zest, cinnamon and a couple of scrapes of nutmeg into a bowl and then add the eggs. Whisk until it comes together and then add to the honey mixture in the jug, combining thoroughly. Pour into the muffin tray and bake for 20 minutes until a skewer inserted through the middle comes out clean. Allow to cool completely.

Make the icing by beating all the ingredients together. Top the cakes with it before finishing off with the flowers.

CHOCOLATE MALTESER CHEESECAKE

It needs no bigger sell than . . . Chocolate Malteser CHEESECAKE!

Serves 6–8

100g white chocolate Maltesers

175g digestive biscuits

90g butter, melted, plus extra for greasing

100g plain chocolate, chopped

100g milk chocolate, chopped

3 tbsp good-quality cocoa powder

3 tbsp hot water

400ml double cream

400g full-fat cream cheese

200g caster sugar

Lightly grease and line the base and sides of a 23cm round springform tin with baking parchment.

Set aside 6–8 Maltesers. Whizz the biscuits and the rest of the Maltesers in a food processor until they are finely crushed. Add the melted butter and blitz until the mixture clumps together. Press into the base of your ready and waiting tin and chill thoroughly in the fridge.

Melt both types of chocolate in a heatproof bowl over a pan of barely simmering water, making sure the base of the bowl doesn't touch the water. When it's melted, lift the bowl off the pan and put it to one side until the chocolate is cool but still liquid. Put the cocoa powder into a small bowl and stir in the hot water to make a smooth mixture. Leave it to cool.

Whip the cream in a large bowl until it just holds its shape, then fold in the cooled melted chocolate and the cocoa powder mix. In another large bowl, beat together the cream cheese and sugar until smooth then fold it into the chocolate cream mixture until well mixed. Spoon the cheesecake mixture on top of the chilled biscuit base, level, and chill until set, which usually takes 3–5 hours, depending on how cold your fridge is. Top with the reserved Maltesers . . . erm, silly question, but anyone for cheesecake?

PROPER CORNISH SCONES

Come on, whisk some up and let's get cosy. Scones + cream + jam = Heaven.
My dad loves them with a hint of cinnamon so I add a teaspoon with the flour.

Makes 5–6

**225g self-raising flour,
plus extra for dusting**

1 tsp baking powder

**40g butter, slightly
softened (but still cool)
and cubed**

1 tbsp caster sugar

pinch of salt

1 large free-range egg

120ml milk

Preheat the oven to 220°C/gas 7.

Sift the flour and baking powder in a large bowl and add the butter.
Then rub the butter and flour together until you have a breadcrumb-like
mixture. Gently stir in the sugar and add the pinch of salt. Now whisk the
egg into the milk and pour into the flour and butter mixture (saving a little
bit in the bottom of the jug to brush the scones with before baking), stirring
it until you have a dough. If the dough is a bit sticky, don't worry, as this
will ensure they rise really well!

Lightly flour a surface and gently roll out the dough until it is 2cm thick.
Then, using a 5cm cutter, cut out your scones (another tip is to push down
and pull up the cutter without twisting it so that the scones rise evenly).
Gather up the leftover dough, roll out again and cut another scone – you
should end up with five or six scones. Pop the scones on a baking tray
and brush with the milky egg mix.

Bake for 10–12 minutes or until pale golden and risen. Then allow them
to cool on a wire rack . . . What am I talking about! Eat them warm with
loads of cream and jam!

DEAD BANANAS CAKE

This oh so banana-ey cake has been named by my girls due to their horror at how black the bananas are that I use. Mind you, it doesn't stop them having slice after slice. You can of course leave the Nutella out of the recipe . . .

Serves 6–8

3 medium-sized very ripe bananas

200g self-raising flour, sifted

160g butter, softened

80g caster sugar

100g chocolate chips

80g chopped roasted hazelnuts

2 free-range eggs

2 tbsp maple syrup or honey

1 tsp vanilla extract

FOR THE TOPPING (OPTIONAL)

3–6 tbsp Nutella

Preheat the oven to 160°C/ gas 3. Grease and line a 450g loaf tin with baking parchment.

Mash the bananas in a bowl then add all the other ingredients and stir until everything is thoroughly mixed. Pour the mixture into the prepared loaf tin and bake for an hour. Once it has cooled completely spread the Nutella on top . . . mmmmm.

PECAN LOAF CAKES

These are a bit special because of the extra faffing about with the candied pecans but they are worth it – for God's sake don't waste them on the kids though.

Makes 6–8

175g self-raising flour

125g butter, softened

2 free-range eggs

150g caster sugar

1 tsp ground cinnamon

2 tbsp maple syrup

splash of milk

FOR THE MAPLE BUTTERCREAM ICING

75g butter, softened

150g icing sugar

1 tsp ground cinammon

2 tbsp maple syrup

FOR THE CANDIED NUTS

3 tbsp caster sugar

big pinch of salt

12 pecan nuts

Preheat the oven to 180°C/gas 4 and line a tray with mini loaf cases.

For the candied nuts, heat the sugar, salt and nuts in a heavy-based pan, stirring with a wooden spoon, until the sugar turns sticky. Heat for a couple more minutes until the sugar melts. Once the sugar has completely melted, tip the nuts onto baking parchment and allow to cool.

Put all the cake ingredients in a processor and jooge a couple of times. Then, using a spatula, scrape the sides down before jooging again. Now divide the mixture equally into the mini loaf cases and bake for about 25–30 minutes or until a skewer that you've inserted comes out clean. Leave them to cool for a few minutes, then remove the cases from the tray to continue cooling on a rack.

Whisk together the icing ingredients. When the cakes are cool, ice them and decorate with the candied nuts.

CUTESY CAKE POPS

Honestly, promisely, your kids will beam with pride at the wonder of you as you make your entrance into any party with these cake pops held aloft! Let's hear it for the mums – or dads!

You will need a silicone cake pop mould, available online and in some kitchen shops. If you fancy a citrus flavour, you can add lemon or orange zest. If you think you'd prefer chocolate cake, just substitute 2 tablespoons of flour with 2 of sifted cocoa powder.

Makes 20

100g butter, softened, plus extra for greasing

100g caster sugar

3 free-range eggs, lightly whisked

100g self-raising flour, plus extra for dusting

TO DECORATE

200g of your favourite chocolate

20 pop or lolly sticks

sprinkles or finely chopped nuts

Preheat the oven to 180°C/gas 4. Brush a little melted butter or oil into your mould, then dust with a little flour.

Beat together the butter and sugar until light and fluffy. Then add the eggs slowly, whisking the whole time. Sift the flour and fold in until thoroughly combined. Now spoon the batter into one side of the mould and then put the other side on top. Bake for 20 minutes.

Take out of the oven, remove the top mould and allow the pops to cool. Then take them out of the mould and lay them on a baking tray lined with baking parchment.

Melt the chocolate in a small bowl over a lightly simmering pan of water. Do NOT let the bowl touch the water or allow any water into the chocolate as it will spoil and your only option will be to start all over again!

Once the chocolate has melted, take it off the heat but leave it over the pan of warm water to keep it liquid. Dip the end of a cake pop stick into the melted chocolate, push the stick 90% of the way into one of the cake pops then stand it back on the baking tray. Repeat until they are all done. If you want, you can now pop the cakes in the freezer for half an hour to firm them up a bit (and avoid any disasters) but I will admit I don't bother (am soooo impatient) and they work out fine.

Now hold each pop over the bowl of melted chocolate and spoon the chocolate over the pop. Sprinkle with your sprinkles or nuts and then stand the pops up (I stick them in a piece of polystyrene but you could stand them in a short glass). Allow to set and then hand out to all those you love!

LEMON CURD BAKEWELL TART

I invented this tart for my friend and agent Neil, as he is a registered lemon curd addict and wherever there is jam called for in a recipe he wants lemon curd instead (it can be exhausting!). He tried rehab a couple of times but on his release he fell off the wagon and was back on the curd within hours . . . It's all been very sad.

Serves 6

FOR THE PASTRY

(You can use shop-bought pastry, but it won't be as nice!)

125g plain flour, sifted, plus extra for dusting

50g butter, slightly softened (but still cool) and cubed

45g icing sugar, sifted

1 free-range egg, at room temperature

2 drops of almond extract

FOR THE FILLING

50g unsalted butter, softened

35g caster sugar

50g ground almonds

3–4 drops of almond extract

1 dsp plain flour, sifted

6 tbsp lemon curd

Grease a loose-bottomed 20cm tin.

Put the flour in a bowl, make a well and drop the butter and icing sugar into the middle. Using your fingertips, blend quickly and lightly until you have a grainy texture. Then make another well and add the egg and almond extract. Again, mix together with your fingertips until you have a smooth dough. Wrap the pastry in clingfilm and pop into the fridge for a couple of hours.

Roll out the pastry on a floured surface and lay into the prepared tin. Prick all over with a fork. Put back in the fridge for 30 minutes (this is really important so the pastry doesn't shrink).

Preheat the oven to 180°C/gas 4.

Line the pastry with baking parchment and then pour in baking beans. Bake for 8 minutes. Take out of the oven, remove the paper and beans, pop back into the oven and bake for another 5–7 minutes until lightly golden. Allow to cool.

To make the filling, beat the butter and sugar together, using an electric whisk, until light and fluffy and then stir in the other ingredients apart from the lemon curd. Spoon the lemon curd into the pastry case and then top with the almond mixture. Bake for 30–40 minutes or until lightly golden.

STUPIDLY EASY STRAWBERRY CHEESECAKE

Come on, anyone can do this, anyone, even my cat! And it looks so pretty too. You will need one plate and two forks.

Serves 2

1 tbsp icing sugar

1 tsp vanilla extract

100g full-fat cream cheese

1 tbsp strawberry jam

6 strawberries, chopped

4 light digestive biscuits

Beat together the icing sugar, vanilla extract and cream cheese with an electric whisk and then swirl in the jam.

Now layer the cream cheese mixture and strawberries between the digestive biscuits, and then put on a serving plate. Believe me, it is yum!

SOD-THE-DIET CAKE!

Look at the photograph, read the title . . . need I say more?

Serves 6–8

Serves 6–8

200g butter, softened

3 large free-range eggs

180g self-raising flour, sifted

20g cocoa powder

200g caster sugar

1 tbsp baking powder

2 tbsp milk

60g white chocolate chunks

60g milk chocolate chunks

FOR THE BUTTERCREAM

125g butter, softened

225g icing sugar

4 tbsp cocoa powder

1–2 tbsp milk

TO DECORATE

6 chocolate flakes

chocolate sprinkles

Preheat the oven to 180°C/gas 4. Grease and line two 20cm cake tins.

To make the cake, put the butter, eggs, flour, cocoa powder, sugar and baking powder into a large bowl and whisk together. Only add the milk when it feels stiff – the mixture should drop off a spoon. Now slowly fold in the chocolate chunks. Spoon into the prepared tins.

Place in the preheated oven and bake for around 25 minutes. You'll know they're done when they're springy to the touch and have shrunk from the sides. Leave them for a couple of minutes, then remove from the tins and allow to cool completely on a wire rack.

To make the buttercream, put the softened butter, icing sugar and cocoa in a bowl and beat until fluffy. Add the milk and stir – you should add a little bit more if it feels a bit stiff. Spread half of it on the top of each cake and sandwich together. Next, top with the crumbled flakes and the chocolate sprinkles.

APRICOT TARTE TATIN

Nicky Johnston – photographer to the stars – this one's for you. And yes, tarte Tatin really does mean 'upside-down tart'!

Serves 6

You will need a small heavy-based ovenproof frying pan, roughly 20cm diameter

80g caster sugar

50g butter

300g fresh apricots, halved and stoned

1 x 375g pack all-butter, ready-rolled puff pastry (that was a mouthful)

2 tbsp chopped, roasted hazelnuts

2 tsp icing sugar

Put the sugar into the frying pan and melt it over a medium heat until it caramelizes and turns a nice golden brown. However tempting, don't stir it, but you can swirl it around in the pan.

Now take the melted sugar off the heat and stir in the butter. Be really careful, as the caramel will be as hot as molten lava. Stir for a couple of minutes until it thickens and becomes smooth. Once it looks like smooth toffee, pop the apricots on top, skin side down, and set to one side for half an hour or so. Basically you want it to cool down enough so as not to melt the pastry!

Preheat the oven to 200°C/gas 6. Set your pastry on a floured surface and roll it out until it's a little wider than your frying pan – I use a 25cm plate at this point to cut round the pastry.

Lay the pastry on top of the apricots and, using a knife, push it gently around the edges of the fruit. Prick all over with a fork (this is to allow the steam out) and bake for 25–30 minutes until the pastry is golden brown.

Take the tatin out of the oven and let it sit for 5 minutes, then gently loosen the edges by running a knife round. Put a plate on top of your pan and turn it over so that your tart lands on the plate! Before serving, sprinkle with the chopped hazelnuts and icing sugar. Serve with cream or ice cream.

PERFECT PEAR AND FRANGIPANE TART

This is one of my dad's favourite (there are so many) desserts. I think he does a grand job of conning himself into believing that any pud with fruit in it is good for him!! Well of course that's the case . . . especially with lots of cream!

Serves 6

FOR THE PASTRY

250g plain flour, sifted

100g butter, slightly softened (but still cool) and cubed

90g icing sugar, sifted

2 free-range eggs, at room temperature

1 tsp vanilla extract

FOR THE FRANGIPANE FILLING

100g unsalted butter, softened

70g caster sugar

1 heaped tbsp plain flour

5 drops of almond extract

100g ground almonds

4 ripe pears, peeled, cored and halved

Grease a loose-bottomed 20cm tin.

Put the flour in a bowl, make a well and drop the butter and icing sugar into the middle. Using your fingertips, work the ingredients quickly and lightly until you have an almost grainy texture. Then make another well and add the eggs and vanilla. Using your fingertips mix together until you have a smooth dough. Wrap the pastry in clingfilm and pop into the fridge for a couple of hours.

Roll out half the pastry on a floured surface to 2mm thickness and lay into the prepared tin. Prick all over with a fork. Put back in the fridge for 30 minutes (this is really important so the pastry doesn't shrink).

Preheat the oven to 180°C/gas 4.

Line the pastry with baking parchment and then pour in baking beans. Bake for 8 minutes. Take out of the oven, remove the paper and beans, pop back into the oven and bake for another 5–7minutes until lightly golden.

Now for the filling. Using an electric whisk beat the butter and sugar together until creamy. Then whisk in all the rest of the ingredients except for the pears. Spoon the mixture into the pastry case but not right to the top (you can sometimes be left with a little of the frangipane mixture) and arrange the pears on top. Score the pears with a sharp knife if you want a pretty, ridged effect.

Bake for 30–40 minutes or until puffed up and golden. Serve warm with cream or ice cream – not both, Dad!

AND
NOW FOR
SOMETHING
SWEET

Sweet: *adjective* having the pleasant taste characteristic of sugar or honey; something delightful . . . I couldn't agree more!

When it comes to a full-blown three-course meal (ahhh, how I love those words), I can easily pass on the starter. OK, maybe not quite so easily, but I certainly wouldn't dissolve into tears at the dining table (well, I'd hope not). In fact, at a push, if you paid me, bribed me or threatened me, I could even possibly be forced to forgo my main meal (so long as I could have a couple of sessions, there and then at the table, with a top psychiatrist). But, when it comes to sweet things – dessert, pud, afters, my REWARD for living – I really couldn't be held responsible for my actions if I were forced to go without it!

I can unashamedly say that for me and all my brood, this final course is the 'ahhh' moment of any meal, and pretty much the 'ahhh' moment of day-to-day living! The sweet is the grand finale to a fabulous show – the final hoorah! Everything else has been building up to this tasty moment. It's when the eyes bulge, the tummy rumbles in anticipation and one really wants to over-indulge!

Without wishing to sound too easy to please, I can't think of a single time I've been presented with a dessert I didn't like! From the poshest of Michelin-starred mousses to the most meagre pud of bananas and custard, each and every one of them has tickled my fancy in just the way I've wanted them to.

So here follow some of my favourite desserts – it was a hard choice to make, but I hope you love them as much as I do!

BLACKBERRY, APPLE AND ALMOND COBBLER

I love cooking with pick-your-own fruit as it allows me to channel Mrs Beeton, bonnet an' all! Now, where can I find some blackberries . . . Nanny Thelma, I'm on my way to yours!

Serves 4–6

6 eating apples

200g blackberries

1 tbsp caster sugar for sprinkling

FOR THE COBBLER

60g plain flour, sifted

1 tsp baking powder

30g ground almonds

2 tsp ground cinnamon (optional)

80g soft brown sugar

100ml Greek yogurt

60g butter, melted

FOR THE TOPPING

handful of whole roasted almonds

Preheat the oven to 180°C/gas 4.

Peel, core and quarter the apples, put them in a saucepan with a couple of tablespoons of water and simmer for 3–4 minutes until softened. Lay them in a dish and top with the blackberries. Then sprinkle a little caster sugar over the blackberries.

Put all the cobbler ingredients into a mixing bowl and give them a good stir. Then spoon the batter on top of the fruit. Sprinkle with the whole almonds and bake for 30–40 minutes until the top is golden and the fruit is bubbling. Serve warm with cream or custard.

CANOFFEE PIE

I am so annoyed with the utterly naff name I have given this pie but once you have read the recipe you will see I had no choice!

Serves 6–8

FOR THE BASE

250g chocolate Hobnobs (I know, soooo sinful)

100g butter, plus extra for greasing

FOR THE FILLING

397g can Carnation caramel

FOR THE TOPPING

250ml double cream

1 tsp espresso instant coffee made with 1 dsp boiling water

2 tbsp icing sugar

sweet coffee beans and 2 chocolate flakes, to decorate

Grease a 20cm loose-bottomed cake tin.

Blitz the biscuits in a blender until they are crumbs. Melt the butter, add it to the biscuit crumbs and mix well. Now line the base of the cake tin with the biscuit mixture, pushing down well with the back of a spoon. Pop it into the fridge for half an hour.

Pour the caramel onto the biscuit base and put back in the fridge.

When you are ready to serve, remove the cake from the tin. Next, whisk the double cream with the coffee and icing sugar until thickened. Pile on top of the canoffee pie and decorate with sweet coffee beans and crumbled chocolate flakes.

MARK'S ONCE A YEAR JAMMY TARTS

I am going to admit (with my head hung in shame) that I am more than a little jealous of how delicious my Mark's pastry is. He has the 'gift', so I make sure he doesn't get to make it more than once a year! When he is allowed in the kitchen these are the gorgeously jammy, buttery tarts that result!

Makes 8 individual tarts

FOR THE PASTRY

350g plain flour, sifted, plus extra for dusting

160g roasted hazelnuts, blitzed until fine

100g icing sugar

finely grated zest of 2 large lemons

1 tsp ground cinnamon

200g cold butter, cubed, plus extra for greasing

2 large free-range eggs and 1 yolk, beaten

FOR THE FILLING

300g raspberry jam

zest of 1 lemon

2 tbsp lemon juice

You will need 8x6cm loose-bottomed fluted pie tins, lightly greased and floured

Put all the pastry ingredients except the eggs in a bowl and rub together with your fingers until it's like a crumble. Then, using a knife, mix in the eggs. Wrap in clingfilm and put it in the fridge for 30 minutes.

Preheat the oven to 190°C/gas 5. Put a heavy baking tray into the oven and let it get nice and hot.

Flour your surface and gently roll out the pastry into 8 x 6cm circles about 0.5cm thick, then carefully lift them into the tin. You want the pastry to come up slightly higher than the edge of the tins.

Now mix the filling ingredients together in a jug and pour onto your beautifully prepared pastry bases. Make a lattice with the leftover pastry and lay on top of the jammy filling. Put the pies on the hot baking tray and cook until the pastry is golden – this will take about 18–25 minutes.

When cooked, remove from the oven and allow to cool. I suggest serving with a big dollop of cream!

SO EASY IT SHOULDN'T BE ALLOWED ICE CREAM!

I love good-quality homemade ice cream as much as the next glutton, but sometimes I just can't be bothered to hang about stirring custard and listening to the whirring of the ice-cream machine for hours. There is no substitute for really good-quality ice cream but, for the amount of work involved, this comes pretty blooming close.

Serves 6

250ml best-quality ready-made custard

250ml double cream

3 tsp vanilla extract

1 tsp rosewater extract

4 tbsp icing sugar

80g rosewater Turkish delight, roughly chopped (best quality possible)

pomegranate molasses, to serve

Put the custard, double cream, vanilla and rosewater extract and icing sugar into a large bowl and, using an electric whisk, whisk until the mixture becomes thick and loosely holds its own weight. This can take quite a bit of whisking – don't lose faith, it will happen.

Add the Turkish delight pieces to the mixture and fold with a large spoon or spatula to incorporate. Pour the mixture into a plastic pot that has a tight-fitting lid. Place in the freezer and leave for 2 hours.

After 2 hours take the ice cream from the freezer and, using a spoon, mix the frozen bits from around the outside with the unfrozen in the middle. Replace in the freezer and leave for a minimum of 6 hours, but preferably overnight.

Remove the ice cream from the freezer about 10 minutes before wanting to serve. Serve huge scoops drizzled with pomegranate molasses.

COCONUT ICE

My mum made this with her mum, I made it with my mum, and my girls make it with me, and so it will continue long after we are all gone . . .

250ml condensed milk

1 tbsp vanilla extract

225g icing sugar, sifted, plus extra for dusting

200g desiccated coconut

pink food colouring

Put the condensed milk and vanilla extract into a pan and heat gently, stirring constantly, until just simmering, then set aside for 45 minutes.

Stir the icing sugar and coconut together in a bowl, then pour in the milk and mix well.

Divide the mixture in half and put into separate bowls. Add a few drops of pink food colouring to one of the bowls and work through until evenly coloured.

Dust a work surface with icing sugar and shape the white dough into a rough rectangle about 1.5cm thick. Do the same with the pink dough and place on top. Put onto a piece of parchment paper on a board and leave to set at room temperature overnight.

Cut into squares and share with those you love!

MINI TROPICAL PAVLOVAS

My beautiful, precious step-daughters, Issy and Fleur, love my pavlova but they adore these babies as they get a whole one to themselves!

Makes 6

2 free-range egg whites

120g caster sugar

1 tsp white wine vinegar

1 tsp vanilla extract

1 tsp cornflour

200ml double cream

150ml coconut cream

1 large mango, peeled, stoned and cubed

2 ripe kiwis, peeled and chopped

Preheat the oven to 150°C/gas 2.

Put the egg whites into a clean bowl and whisk. Start at a low speed and then gradually increase until you get soft peaks. Don't overwhisk as this will cause the whites to collapse. Now add the sugar a tablespoon at a time, whisking continuously until you have a shiny glossy stiff mixture, then whisk in the vinegar, vanilla and cornflour.

Spoon into six individual mounds on a non-stick baking tray. Make an indentation in each one with the back of a spoon. Pop into the oven and bake for 1 hour. Turn off the heat and leave the meringue in the oven until it cools right down. Then whip the double cream and coconut cream together and fill the meringues with it. Decorate with the fruit.

PISTACHIO BISCUITS

I dare you to show me an easier recipe for biscuits as delicious as this. Go on, I dare you!
  PS They are also wheat-free!

Makes 10

90g pistachios, finely ground

100g ground almonds

90g caster sugar

½ tsp almond extract

1 large free-range egg white

100g pistachios, roughly chopped

Preheat the oven to 180°C/gas 4.

  Put the finely ground pistachios, almonds, sugar, almond extract and egg white in a bowl and give them a really good mix. Form the mixture into small balls and flatten them slightly with the palm of your hand. Now roll them in the chopped pistachios and pop on a baking tray, leaving space between each. Bake for 10–13 minutes, then allow to cool on the baking tray.

RHUBARB FOOL WITH CRUMBLE TOPPING

This dessert will satisfy all your senses. The sharpness of the baked rhubarb is perfectly cushioned by the mallow sweetness of the meringue-enriched cream (blimey, went all Nigella there!).

Serves 4–6 (depending on the size of the glass)

200g plain flour, sifted

100g cold butter, cubed

225g caster sugar

4 tbsp chopped roasted hazelnuts

400g rhubarb, chopped into 3–4cm chunks

1 orange, zest and juice

3 free-range egg whites

200ml double cream, whipped to soft peaks

Preheat your oven to 180°C/gas 4.

Place the flour and butter in a bowl and, using a rubbing action with your fingers, combine the two until you have a breadcrumb consistency. Add 75g sugar and the hazelnuts, and mix until all the ingredients are combined. Tip onto a flat baking tray and evenly distribute. Place in the preheated oven and bake for about 15 minutes. Keep an eye on the mix as the outside will colour much quicker than the centre. When cooked, remove from the oven and leave to cool.

Place the chopped rhubarb in a baking dish. Grate the zest of the orange over the rhubarb, before squeezing the juice over the top. If the orange you are using is dry, add a couple of tablespoons of water. Sprinkle over 60g sugar and place the dish in the oven. Bake for 10–12 minutes, by which time the rhubarb should be soft but holding its shape. When cooked, remove from the oven and allow to cool completely.

Place your egg whites in a clean bowl and whisk (I highly recommend an electric whisk!) until the whites have more than doubled in size and are lovely and frothy. Add a tablespoon of sugar and whisk again until the sugar is worked in and the egg whites begin to look slightly glossy. Add 2 more tablespoons of sugar and, again, whisk in thoroughly. You can add a bit more sugar each time, before whisking in fully. By now the egg whites should have taken on a stiff texture and a silky, glossy appearance.

Add a third of your whisked egg white mix to the whipped cream and whisk in until fully incorporated. Dollop in the remaining two-thirds and, using a spoon or spatula and a folding and chopping motion, gently incorporate the egg white into the cream. Try to be both gentle and persuasive!

Divide the creamy mixture between your glasses and, along with the cooked and cooled rhubarb, place in the fridge for at least 30 minutes.

Remove the glasses from the fridge and spoon some rhubarb onto each one, before breaking up the cooked crumble and sprinkling over the tops.

DELICIOUS DONNA

Linda, Lee and Donna are the wonderful make-up artists who put us all together for *Loose Women* and they are all blooming lovely! Donna is extra lovely, though (sorry, Lind and Lee!), because she makes us all these super-delicious, super-healthy sweet bites, that we can nibble away on whilst we are rebuilt!

Makes 12–15

2 tbsp coconut oil

2 handfuls of porridge oats

handful of milled flaxseeds

2 tbsp raw cocoa powder

handful of raw cocoa nibs

handful of mixed nuts and seeds (Donna uses: linseeds, pumpkin, sunflower, goji berries, chia, coconut flakes, flaked almonds)

very big splash of vanilla extract

maple syrup

100g dark chocolate, 85% cocoa solids

Line a small baking tray with greaseproof paper.

Melt the coconut oil in a large saucepan. Remove from the heat and add all the other ingredients except the maple syrup and chocolate and mix thoroughly. Add maple syrup, a tablespoon at a time, stirring until it starts binding together. Flatten the mixture onto the prepared baking tray.

Melt the dark chocolate in a bowl over a pan of simmering water and drizzle over the top.

Put in the fridge overnight. Once set, cut into squares.

NANNY GLENDA'S FRIDGE CAKE

Now my nan's name was Gladys, but she hated her name with a passion . . . so I have righted the wrong and renamed her Glenda. She would have loved it!

Makes 25 squares

200g raisins

150ml rum (or orange juice if you think the kids will get a look-in)

200g light digestive biscuits

100g dark chocolate

200g milk chocolate

120g butter, at room temperature, plus extra for greasing

1 tbsp golden syrup

1 free-range egg yolk

50g glacé cherries, chopped

100g salted peanuts, roughly chopped

Grease a 20cm square brownie tin and line with baking parchment.

Put the raisins in a small saucepan with the rum and heat very gently until they have absorbed most of the liquid. Leave to cool.

Put the biscuits into a plastic bag and bash into small pieces with a rolling pin.

Break both chocolates into pieces and put in a heatproof bowl above, but not touching, a pan of simmering water, until the chocolate has melted. Then take it off the heat and allow it to cool a bit.

Meanwhile, put the butter in a bowl with the syrup and beat them together until they're soft and a bit fluffy. Then beat in the egg yolk. Beat the chocolate into the butter mixture, then add the raisins (drain off any excess rum first), biscuit pieces and the rest of the ingredients and give it a good stir. Spoon the mixture into your baking tin and press down firmly with the back of a spoon to make it as flat as possible.

Put in the fridge and once it is solid (this will depend on how cold your fridge is, but overnight should do the trick) cut into squares. Lovely with a glass of cold milk!

A SPOONFUL OF HEAVEN

This is a brilliant emergency pud as it's quite likely you will already have the ingredients or ones that you could swap them for! It's also one of those recipes where you can shove a glass of wine into the hand of one of your guests (the one that turned up early!) and get them to whizz it up for you . . . *très* clever, eh! Or, if you're super-organized you can make them a day ahead.

Serves 6

6 tbsp tangerine marmalade or normal marmalade

75ml water

150g ginger nut biscuits

40g butter, melted

125g crème fraiche

125g mascarpone

80g stem ginger, diced and finely chopped

3 free-range egg whites

90g caster sugar

Put the marmalade into a small pan along with 75ml water and heat the mixture without boiling it. Give the marmalade a good mix as it heats just to loosen it up. Take the pan off the heat and leave to cool.

Roughly break up the ginger nuts into a food processor and blitz to a crumb. With the machine still running, pour in the melted butter and let the processor run for a further 10 seconds so that the butter and biscuits are well mixed. Take six glasses (I find whisky-style tumblers work perfectly), and divide the mixture equally amongst them. Use your fingers to compact the crumbs into the base of your glasses. Leave to one side.

Put the crème fraiche, mascarpone and stem ginger into a large bowl and beat together until smooth – this takes a bit of elbow grease. If you like the flavour of stem ginger, add a drizzle of the syrup too. Place this mix to one side.

Put your egg whites in a clean bowl and whisk (I advise an electric whisk or you'll be there all day) until the whites have more than doubled in size and are lovely and frothy. Add a tablespoon of sugar and whisk again until the sugar is worked in and the egg whites begin to look slightly glossy. Add 2 more tablespoons and again whisk in thoroughly. You can add a bit more sugar each time, before whisking in fully. Keep going until you have incorporated all of the sugar into the egg whites, which should by now have a stiff texture and a silky, glossy look.

Spoon a third of the whisked egg whites into the mascarpone mixture and whisk in thoroughly. Dollop the remaining egg white into the bowl with a spoon. Now use a metal spoon or a spatula and, with a chopping and turning motion, fold the egg white mix in. Try to be gentle yet thorough. The key is to try to keep as much air as possible. (If you've never done this before there are really good little films on YouTube that will show you how!)

When you are happy with the mixture, divide it between the glasses, spooning it on top of the ginger nut biscuit base. Put in the fridge for a minimum of 20 minutes before removing and spooning over equal amounts of the cooled marmalade.

Place them back in the fridge for at least 30 minutes, by which time they will be chilled and firm enough to eat.

Index

Note: page numbers in **bold** refer to recipe photographs.

Acknowledgements

All my love and gratitude to my Mr – you truly are a polymath. Just when I thought I'd witnessed ALL your talents, you take the most beautiful photos for this book without even breaking into a sweat. PS. You look pretty hot too!

All the loveage in the world to my precious friend Miranda. You put your heart and soul into this book with your brilliant styling and every page is how I dreamed it would be. Please, please work with me on every book I ever do! PS. How we laughed. PPS. Loved all the clearing up/eating . . .

I can't imagine how I can thank my dear friend and agent, Neil Howarth, enough for his expertise and dedication (with cake maybe?) There's simply not another agent like him in the world! Thank you thank you thank you! Xx

A huge thank you to my publisher Pan Macmillan (sooooo cool saying that!) and especially to Ingrid Connell who has put up with my upside down, inside out way of working, with her warm smile and a listening ear. Let's do it again!!

Thank you to my designer Lucy Parissi for all her hard work and creativity – the book is beautiful. And to Tania Wilde and Laura Carr for their eagle eyes on the words.

A big thank you to my vast family that stretches across towns, countries and continents. I love you all . . . Even those of you I don't particularly like!

A huge thank you to Julia Alger and Rob Allison, two of the best home ecs in the business and damn fine people to boot! Big kisses x

A massive thank you also to Nicky Johnston for not only being a brilliant photographer but also for making me howl with laughter through every shoot! #thereisnoinsultlikeanickyinsult. And a big thanks to Matt Monfredi for being so lovely and a damn fine assistant to the nutter that is Nicky.

And finally a big big thank you to my dear dear friends Simone Vollmer and Fi – thank you for my beauty you keep it in your bags! (Don't worry, they know what I mean . . . !)